MY FATHER'S BUSINESS

MY FATHER'S BUSINESS

A PRIEST IN FRANCE

BY ABBÉ MICHONNEAU

HERDER AND HERDER

THIS ENGLISH TRANSLATION BY

EDMUND GILPIN

IS BASED ON THE ORIGINAL VERSION OF "LE CURÉ",

PUBLISHED BY LIBRAIRIE ARTHÈME FAYARD, PARIS, 1954

SECOND IMPRESSION PUBLISHED 1959 BY

HERDER AND HERDER, INC.,

7 WEST 46th STREET, NEW YORK 36, N.Y.

NIHIL OBSTAT: ADRIANUS VAN VLIET, S. T. D.

CENSOR DEPUTATUS

IMPRIMATUR: E. MORROGH BERNARD.

VIC. GEN.

WESTMONASTERII, DIE XXa MAII, 1959

LIBRARY OF CONGRESS CATALOG CARD NUMBER: 59—10890

© 1959 BY HERDER KG

MADE AND PRINTED BY HERDER DRUCK, FREIBURG,

WEST GERMANY

LIST OF CONTENTS

PREFACE

THERE was a time when, in every French parish, the people would have been either for or against their priest. If I had written this book in those days, I would have had to cast it into an apologetic mould. My readers would have been those people who normally read pious books, and no one else would have been interested.

Nowadays, anti-clericalism is only a shadow of its former self. It is not entirely dead. People are not constantly up in arms against their parish priest; on the contrary, they tend to be unconscious of his existence. At the present time there are great numbers of people who have absolutely no contact at all with any priest. In many large towns, or at least in certain quarters of such towns, the sight of a man in a cassock is something abnormal. In some country districts, the whole population goes through life without once calling in a priest.

Ignorance can, of course, be part of a wilful attitude of indifference, implying at least a measure of contempt. In our time, however, ignorance of religion is quite often less voluntary; it can be the result of education and living conditions. This is borne out by the fact that religious questions, when raised in the cinema and the popular press, do cause considerable interest. A film with a religious

7

message always attracts attention, and journalists almost cut each other's throats to be first in reporting some religious function and getting hold of photos of the more interesting members of the Church. Religious themes intrigue the public precisely because they are so mysterious – because they cause reactions deep down in people's souls of a sort which they rarely experience. Whether we will or no, these questions touch upon all the most fundamental of our problems. They cast a light on the secret side of our nature, and it is a relief to be able to shed some of our darkness.

If this little book should fall into the hands of a reader who is looking for that lightening of soul, and he should find it here, even though no one else found it of any use, I shall be glad that I took the trouble to write it. Some people will not expect to find much in it. They will treat it like one of those old magazines that one picks up to while away a dreary half hour, perhaps in a spirit of mild curiosity ("Whatever can he have to say about anything as old fashioned as that?"). For these dilettanti it may be like a door that opens on to another world. I have had them very much in mind as I wrote, and I have tried to be as simple and as interesting as I could, hoping to hold their attention. If they have the patience to read it through to the end, they will at least realize that a priest's life is no dilettante existence, and that I had a serious aim in writing it.

Our Lord's words to Nathaniel, "You would not have looked for me if you had not already found me", could be written on the title page of any book. It is very rarely that we open a book about which we know absolutely nothing. That is because we are not interested in anything about which we are entirely ignorant. Many of my readers will be Christians, some will be my brother priests. They all know what a priest is already. "How can I make a book of this sort interesting for them?" I asked myself. A book that attempts to make a subject assimilable to popular taste cannot be at the same time a work of refined scholarship. To interest people who know nothing about priests, one has to give explanations which, to those who know, will be so many statements of the obvious.

I have been worried all along by the need to write a book which would be interesting, and would therefore necessarily offer some new aspects. All I can hope is that I will be forgiven by those who find me too simple, and those who say I am too complicated. When I was asked to write this book, I was very keen to do it, and at the same time rather disinclined. After all, I had written on the subject before, and I was almost sure to repeat myself. But then, as one gets older, one's opinions become more clearly defined, new aspects are always revealing themselves, and problems develop in the course of time as a result of all sorts of events and circumstances. No author can ever have said the last word about the subject which involves his whole life. His work is never complete. Even when he has produced his book, there are still so many things left unsaid, so many details still to be filled in. And this is why I could not resist the temptation to write another book on matters which I have written about before. Even if there is nothing here but an old man's constant repetition, I feel I shall not have been wasting my time, because I shall have tried to convey, once again, the fact that I believe in the work that priests do.

Chapter One

WHAT IS A PARISH PRIEST?

WHAT is a parish priest? Quite simply, he is a priest who has been given a parish to look after by his bishop. He is *appointed* to his parish, whereas he was *ordained* priest; the distinction is important. When a man is ordained priest, he undergoes a deep change, both spiritual and lasting. He becomes a priest because he has received the sacrament of holy orders. But when, later on, he becomes a *parish* priest, he does so simply because there is a vacancy, and the bishop considers he is the man to fill it. No sacrament, only administration, is involved in his appointment. He is appointed to a parish just as other men are appointed to local government posts. A priest is always a priest, even though he may be too ill to say Mass, or too old to do any work. To be a parish priest, however, one has to be actually in charge of this or that district in this or that diocese.

In those countries that have been Christian for many centuries, the whole territory has long been divided into dioceses, and these in turn into parishes. Every foot of ground belongs to one parish or another, so that everyone can claim to have a parish priest. Where parishes are out of the way, and poor or underpopulated, one priest may be in charge of several parishes. It is not unknown in France for one priest to be looking after as many as twelve or thirteen parishes. None the less, the boundaries of each parish remain intact, awaiting the happy day when they will all have priests of their own.

In mission countries, on the other hand, there is often no such division in parishes. The missioners travel over wide areas, with no one assigned to any fixed limits. One might compare them to a small number of harvesters reaping as best they can in a vast acreage, whereas in countries which already possess (at least nominally) an old Christian culture, the mission field is divided into neat patches, each with its own appointed harvester.

If the parish is a large one, the priest will probably be given an assistant priest or priests. These are the curates. He does not choose them, for they, like himself, are appointed by the bishop. He cannot take them on or dismiss them as one might an employee. He cannot even complain if they are too frequently changed or moved. He has only a consultative voice in such matters.

Parish priests are appointed by their bishop, and in their parishes they are his representatives, sharing in his authority, and exercising their ministry on his behalf. He acts through them, and they act with him, their authority only coming to them under his jurisdiction. They belong to the larger unit which is the diocese.

A priest does not choose his parish, the bishop chooses him for it. When I was a young curate, I remember that my future was a matter of great concern to my uncles. Whenever I met them on holiday, they would give me valuable advice. Sometimes they would tell me to try and get the parish of X, because there was this and that to be said in its favour. At another time they would bid me consider the advantages of being parish priest at Z, just as though a parish were like a grocer's business or a doctor's practice. Fortunately for everyone, the decisions rest with the bishop alone, who is responsible for ascertaining the capacities of his priests, the needs of the various parishes, and so on, in order that every priest may, as far as possible, get the job for which he is best fitted.

Once a priest is appointed to a parish, he cannot be moved from it, unless he has caused grave scandal or resigns. He may always be sent to another parish, where he will again be in charge. These are the rights of parish priests, which are not, of course, without disadvantages. With the best will in the world one can look upon oneself as indispensable, even irreplaceable. As we get older, we tend to forget that our strength and energy and ability are waning, that we are neither as bright, nor as enterprising as we used to be. And so one finds old priests "encrusted" one might say, to their parishes, through sheer age. A typical example of this was the old priest who baptized me and whom I went to visit when I was a seminarian. He was eighty then, and he said "Oh yes, I shall die in harness, dear boy. There aren't enough priests to go round, so we have to hang on till the end!" His tenacity was rather touching, but too pathetic to be inspiring, as it was meant to be. It is the parish, after all, which is suffering, when its priest insists on remaining until the end. And he is the only one who can't see it.

Although "parish priest" is the title in general use, there are other modes of address. In Brittany he is called "rector", and Bretons who have come to Paris and adopted Parisian ways still betray their place of origin by greeting us as "Rector".

If a parish priest is made the supervisor of an area which comprises several parishes, each with its own parish priest, in other words a deanery – he is called a rural dean, and this office is an addition to that of parish priest. If he is responsible for an even greater area – something corresponding to an electoral division of one of our French "departments" – we call him an archpriest.

When he takes over a parish, the priest is called "the Rector", "the Parish Priest" or "the Dean", and people no longer refer to him by his name. No longer is he "Father X" or "Father Y". His parishoners will know him by no other name than his title, and it will be only close friends and relatives who know his surname. The children who see him every day would be taken aback if they heard someone calling him by his name, and no doubt even a fair number of his flock would not know who was meant. To all he is now "the Parish Priest", just as his predecessors were in the past and his successors will be in the future.

This way of talking about him is in fact the wonderful expression of a profound truth. In the parish, the parish priest is the Church which has named him as her representative: he *is* the Church which is always the same, yesterday, to-day and to-morrow. Indeed, the Church is a reality among men, but by God's power she will go on for ever. What counts in a priest who comes to a parish is not his pedigree, his social class or family background, but his priesthood and what he makes of it, and the way in which he uses his priesthood to develop and nourish the life of his parish. The more a man lets the light of his priesthood shine through him, the more his parish will glow and bloom with life.

"We've got a parish priest", the people say. And what difference does it make if he be tall or short, brown-haired or fair, learned in the sciences or arts, or skilled with his hands, whether he is a commoner or from one of our aristocratic families? These things do not matter at all, provided that he is Christ still present and spreading the gospel, provided that he is the Church in all her vitality and progress, for then he will be "a good parish priest".

Chapter Two

THE PRIESTLY MINISTRY FROM ITS BEGINNINGS TO THE PRESENT DAY

Since it is important that the reader should have some idea of the historical development of the priest's task, we have asked a specialist, Father Henry, O. P., to write the following chapter, without which this book would not be complete.

As far as we can tell from the available manuscripts, the French word *curé* (parish priest) occurs for the first time in the thirteenth century. Ruteboeuf seems to be the first writer to use the word. It was derived from the Latin *curatus,* which was very rarely used, either before or after Ruteboeuf's time. Does this mean that the actual office of parish priest dates back no further than the thirteenth century? Not necessarily. The function could exist with another name, the task involved remaining basically the same. The change of name could come naturally with a change in mentality, circumstances, or social conditions. To discover the history of parish priests, we have to define more precisely just what their function is and what changes were involved in the course of time.

Canon 451, para. 1 of the Code of Canon Law, states: "A parish priest *(parochus)* is the priest, or the moral person to whom a parish is entrusted as his sole charge, his function being to care for souls, under the authority of the ordinary (bishop) of the place." (By "moral person" is implied a collectivity of priests, for instance, members of a religious order, who are treated and considered as one single individual for legislative purposes.) Thus we have a connection between the priest and the parish, and we can only discover what his work is by finding out what a parish is. Canon 216, para. 1, tells us that every diocese must be divided sectionally by territorial boundaries . . . "each determined section has its church, and the faithful living in that section belong to it". The parish priest, or "pastor" (can. 216), who is responsible for the care of souls, is the priest who is put in charge of one or more of these sections of ecclesiastical territory.

The definition as we find it in Canon Law is obviously the result of a long evolution. It means that the bishop is head of a number of particular churches (that is, all those in his diocese, including the cathedral parish and any religious communities dependent on him) and that he looks after these churches by means of intermediaries (the parish priests) with clearly defined functions. But this was not always the case, as we shall see.

In such a brief essay as this, I am only concerned to sketch a general picture of the early history, and the "pre-history" of parish priests. The few facts assembled here are valid for the generality of churches in the west, but there are of course a great many variations in practice, and even actual exceptions. Until the sixteenth century, and to a certain extent even later, we find differences of ecclesiastical custom between one town and its neighbour that last for many years. We find that what is the accepted practice in one district, comes in much later in another. This is, after all, typical of the sporadic character that Christianity often shows. A city can sometimes remain Christian when completely surrounded by pagans: it can, on the other hand, fall back into paganism as the result of a barbarian invasion. As far as the history of the early Church goes, one can never generalize. One can only speak with any pretension to truth by concentrating on determined and documented periods. Therefore I must ask the reader not to be too ready to make general applications from the following remarks.

The Earliest Apostolate

Our Lord chose twelve apostles. "He gave them power and authority over all devils, and to cure diseases, and he sent them to preach the kingdom of God, and to heal the sick" (Luke 9:1–2).

These apostles were filled with the Holy Spirit at Pentecost and they followed the Lord's orders, beginning to preach to all people and nations. Little by little, Christian communities came into existence. The first was at Jerusalem, with St. James as leader. The other apostles, however, and particularly St. Paul, would always be itinerant preachers, founding new churches wherever they went, and leaving them in the hands of an elder, or elders.

Thus the first generations of Christians were familiar with two types of leader in the Church. There was the resident apostle, the leader of a local church, like St. James at Jerusalem, and there were the itinerant apostles like St. Paul and Barnabas who would be heads of a number of churches with no resident apostle. These two types of church existed side by side for two or three generations, but eventually the first type became the normal one. In the second century, the head of each church was one of its actual members. Not until the seventh century does one find a recurrence of the wandering bishop – in Ireland.

When we say that each church had its own head, we could say with equal truth that there was one religious leader to each city. Country districts, it is generally safe to say, were not evangelized before the fourth century. This is certainly true in the West. Not until the Middle Ages, in fact, does one find the rural areas properly christianized. Thus there were no rural churches, only city churches, and the heads of these churches, although known by differing titles, were what we would to-day call bishops. In the first century, owing to the variety of names in use, it is difficult to discover what difference existed between a *presbyter* and an *episcopus*. Gregory of Tours, writing in the sixth century, uses *episcopus* and *sacerdos* equivalently (*In gloria confessorum,* ch. 79). In the East we find the titles *Hegumenos* and *Proestos,* and later, in the West, *Dominus* and even *Papa*.

The importance of these city churches obviously varied according to the number of citizens and the degree of Christianity they had achieved. At Rome, Christians soon became numerous, and although there was only one church there, under one bishop, various so-called *tituli* (titular churches) were established. It would be wrong, however, to consider these as parish churches. In city churches, parishes are not found before the eleventh century. Not all the churches, however, were as imposingly large as that of Rome. In North Africa Christianity covered a multitude of small towns and villages, and there were about a hundred bishops in the territory. In the fourth century there were about five hundred, some of them "Roman" and others Donatist. These bishops would have been more like priests of country parishes than bishops in the present-day sense, although they had, of course, full episcopal powers of ordination and jurisdiction. In the fourth century, and even later, one could not have been the head of a church if one were not a bishop. This is proved by the use of *diocesis* and *parochia* as equivalent terms for a bishop's territory.

Priests who ministered in towns are sometimes referred to (for example, by Sidonius Apollinarius) as "priests of the second rank". They were not bishops, and nowadays we would simply call them priests. They were not heads of churches, and their functions were quite restricted. They lived near the bishop, and assisted him in everything he did. They were his "presbyterium" or council of elders – a sort of church senate. They did not baptize, but they assisted the bishop at solemn baptisms. They did not celebrate Mass on their own, but they concelebrated with the bishop. They did not preach; instead they listened to the bishop preaching, together with the rest of the faithful. They did not give absolution, but they were present with the bishop at the ceremonies at which penitents were reconciled to the Church. Their principal function was, in fact, to accompany the bishop in prayer and public worship, although they did other things, such as visiting the sick, preparing converts for baptism and penitents for reconciliation. For the first three centuries they seem to have been less important people than the deacons, who were the bishop's almoners and social welfare organizers. At Rome it became customary to choose the pope from among the deacons, even though they were not priests and did not concelebrate with the bishop at Mass. They were, technically, in the service of the bishop and the priests.

Possibly it was persecution that brought out the importance of the priestly ministry. If the bishop was in prison or in hiding, he could delegate a priest to baptize and preach in his place, although this did not make the delegate in any sense the head of the church, or "pastor". Thus we have to be careful when speaking of the priests in charge of the titular churches in cities in those early days, for they were not the parish priests of to-day. The titular churches, situated round about the city, had no priest of their own. Their priest was always the bishop, who would come regularly to celebrate Mass with all his priests. This was the custom at Rome for centuries, whereby there was a "station" at each church, enabling the bishop to be the "high priest" for all his people, everywhere, even though he had only one church of his own. If a delegated priest were to celebrate the liturgy in his titular church, he would only do so after having received the *fermentum* of bread consecrated by the bishop.

Country Priests

Country people tended to be neglected in the early days of the apostolate. A countryman in those days was called *paganus* because he belonged to a *pagus,* or village, and he would in fact have been a pagan as we understand the word to-day. However, there were different types of rural society, with different kinds of Christian organization. In North Africa there were village bishops, who were really only parish priests with episcopal powers. In the East, from the third century onwards, we find *chorepiscopi,* or episcopal envoys who took charge of country churches in the bishop's name and under his guidance. They were ordinary pastors, but they had episcopal powers. In the West there were no country bishops or *chorepiscopi,* because the bishop who was head of the church in the city would also look after the Christians in the outlying districts in person. He would found new churches and visit them more or less regularly. He would be in the habit of covering considerable distances, because these churches would often be situated far away from the town. In the fourth and fifth centuries, which witnessed this beginning of missionary activity in rural areas, there were no fixed boundaries to a bishop's territory. Each bishop was guided in this, not by laws, but by his own conscience and his own apostolic zeal. We have the example of Saint Martin of Tours, for instance, who established churches very far from his own town.

Thus it became necessary for the bishop to leave behind him some responsible persons to do his work while he was away, or failing that, to send on a missionary before him to prepare for his coming, and to preach the gospel in his name. In the fifth and sixth centuries these delegates and envoys were rarely priests. They were not called upon to celebrate Mass, or to baptize, or even to reconcile penitents. The bishop still kept his priests about him, and those he sent before him as missionaries were deacons. It was these latter who looked after the churches in rural areas, and they in turn were supervized by an archdeacon, who, like themselves, was not a priest. In the Merovingian period, an archdeacon would have a determined area under his control, comprising a certain number of country churches.

The deacon in charge of a parish was in fact more like a catechist in the mission field to-day. He would prepare the converts for baptism, visit the sick and minister to the needy. He would always be fighting local superstitions, and would need to be constantly exhorting the Christians to lead a good life.

Eventually of course it was natural that these rural communities should have priests of their own. They had their own churches, oratories and votive chapels, and these quite soon became very numerous. They could not at first be called "churches" in the strict sense because they had neither bishop nor priests, but from the sixth century onwards they secured the right to baptize. They then became known as *plebes baptismales* or *ecclesiae*. There came about a gradual decentralization, and quite often new Christian communities were established by laymen. Finally the bishops sent priests, instead of going out to these churches in person. The Mass would be celebrated by a priest with a gathering of the clergy, deacons and those in minor orders. As well as the Mass, baptisms and all other acts of worship were celebrated. A dean was now appointed to look after the country priests, and in some places an archpriest (who must not be confused with the archpriest of the presbyterium).

A country priest in those days was no isolated figure, a priest on his own being something contrary to the early Church's way of thinking. Even in the sixth and seventh centuries, no priest was left on his own, either in the towns or in the country discricts. With his own little group of clerics, he formed a replica of the bishop's urban hierarchy. He would say Mass twice or three times a week, and celebrate a service of morning and evening prayer together with his clergy and some of his people. He and his community would look after the sick and the dying, instructing new converts and future clerics.

There was hardly any difference, in fact, before the ninth century, between these small communities of clerics in the country and the monastic communities which were beginning to appear everywhere. The distinction which we make to-day between "secular" and "regular" clergy was not, at that time, known. The rural clergy, like the monks, often led a life that was half active and half contemplative. The difference between these clerics and the monks was in the precise mode of community life they followed, and the physical austerities which the monks practised. But as far as the divine office went, and the care of souls, one has the impression that all the clergy of that time had much the same functions and the same aspirations. In those days a *monasterium,* or *monasteriolum,* as far as we can gather from extant records, was as much a rural parish as a monastery, at least in its early stages. The functions of parish clergy were not clearly defined, and they took up the religious life rather more for the sake of devoting themselves to the prayer of the church than for the active ministry such as we understand it to-day. Thus it came about, from the seventh century onwards, that many of these colleges of priests or of canons adopted the daily office of seven "hours" to be recited during the day, already in use by the Benedictine monks flourishing in Gaul. Gradually the office which had been used in monastic churches, consisting of morning prayers when there was no Mass, and evening prayers or *lucernarium* (when the lamps were lit), was discontinued.

The various orders in the clergy, and the various types or religious order, were distinguished by the colour and quality of their dress and by the liturgical rites that they followed. Even in the twelfth century such secondary details as these were matter of argument between monks and canons. Monks wore black to denote their penitential way of life, whereas clerics wore white "like the angels who announced Our Lord's resurrection". Thus the monks of Cîteaux gave scandal when they appeared in white habits, until they put forward the explanation that poverty forbade them to wear dyed wool. Monks wore wool, whereas clerics (particularly priests celebrating the liturgy) wore linen.

In the twelfth century, one could recognize a religious community by the liturgy it followed. If it kept the rule and the *ordo* of Saint Benedict, it was monastic and Bene-dictine, for at that time there was no other monastic rule. Saint Benedict's rule had been imposed on all the monks of the Empire by Charlemagne, so that the rule of Saint Columbanus fell into disuse. If a community followed the *ordo* of the bishopric in which it was situated, it was what we should call nowadays "diocesan", but this did not mean that it was any less monastic. It could be dependent on the bishop and at the same time live under a definite rule. This was the case with the canons of Saint Rufus in the eleventh century, and the Premonstraten-sians in the twelfth. Besides, not all the monks were exempt, as we say to-day, from the bishop's authority. The liturgy could vary from one bishopric to another (despite the various efforts made during the tenth and eleventh centuries to bring about liturgical unity) and between one community and another in the same diocese. The twelfth-century liturgies are much more clear-cut and stable than those of the seventh century. One can, with a little practice, distinguish them from each other and give them a name, which is far from being the case in the earlier period. As Laugardière says, "country parishes in those days were like little monasteries. The way of perfection was not thought of as an exclusive devotion to the interior life, without outside activity. A cleric of the seventh century was at the same time a monk, a pastor, and a missionary. A monk was always potentially, and often in fact, an apostle. This was the tradition of Saint Martin. Clerics and monks were brothers to each other, and were known to be such by everyone. This was a far cry from any modern conception of a parish. . . ."

But, as we have already observed, there were degrees of importance among the churches of the country districts. Those which were governed by a deacon, for instance, had less prestige than those which had several priests with an "archpresbyter" over them. The latter type carried out, although on a less solemn scale, all the rites observed in a bishop's church. The simple fact that a church had a baptistery was enough, in the fifth and sixth centuries, to allow it to be considered almost equal in rank with an episcopal church, but this was not so with the many little country churches staffed by a few priests or deacons. For the clergy in these outlying districts it was still necessary to come into the city for all great feasts – Easter, Christmas, and Pentecost, for instance, and all solemn liturgical occasions. We can hardly imagine a present-day bishop convening all his clergy, bar the deans, from all his parishes to concelebrate with him at Easter. But that is in fact what happened in Gaul from the sixth to the eighth centuries. The fifteenth canon of the council of Clermont (A.D. 535) lays down that "priests and deacons not belonging to the episcopal church or to the parishes (and here the word *parochia* is used with almost the same sense which we give it to-day), but serving the oratories in country districts, are to come and celebrate with the bishop on the aforementioned feasts." The same obligation applies to the *cives natu majores* – which may have meant the whole adult population, or only those of noble blood.

Such legislation shows a certain conception of the relations existing between bishop and priests. During the Middle Ages, the only person who corresponds to our present-day parish priest is, paradoxically, the bishop. He was the city's parish priest. Every Sunday he would celebrate Mass surrounded by his clergy. He would reconcile the penitents, preach, instruct the people, and baptize.

He would also be concerned with certain temporal affairs, such as pleas, contracts, enfranchisements, judgements, etc. The temporal was extremely involved in the spiritual, and a bishop would often become a person of importance in civil life. In Charlemagne's time he was a temporal lord with his own vassals although primarily a pastor, and his administrative work was comparatively restricted. In those days there were no curial offices for diocesan business. Not until the twelfth and thirteenth centuries do we find vicars-general, notaries, secretaries and the like, because it was not until then that the old presbyterium gave place to the cathedral chapter.

The fact that a bishop would be technically in charge of other parishes as well as his own city parish suggests a comparison with some present-day priests who have several parishes in their care. In either case one parish is singled out as the most important, and kept for normal residence. The others tend to be poor relations. This helps us to see quite clearly that a bishop, in those days, was primarily the pastor in his own town, and not the administrator of a large diocese. He was a parish priest among other parish priests, and not a senior ecclesiastic in charge of, and remote from, all the parishes and priests. A bishop then had a parish of his own for which he was responsible, besides being superior in rank to all other priests dependent on him. It was not until the eleventh century that a great change came about, causing the bishop to be cut off from his people. Towns were divided up into several parishes for the first time. This resulted in the situation that we find to-day, in which all parishes, whether urban or rural, are more or less independent entities. Each is dependent on its own priest. The bishop is not a pastor, but the head of a group of pastors. In each community, the mass, baptism, confession, preaching, and the general church organization of the faithful are the business of the parish priest alone. The old system of church-visiting by archdeacons and *chorepiscopi* fell into disuse. Parish priests became more independent, as they were less closely bound to the bishop. The extreme implication of this situation is that some priests cannot be removed from their parishes even by the bishop.

From the sixth century onwards there are occasional instances of priests living alone, but their rarity is accounted for by the fact that their position did not please either the bishops or the councils of the Church. Custom and rule had always laid down that clerics should live in communities, as numerous as possible. This was indeed the practice in country districts, where priests and deacons always had the clergy in minor orders about them to give more solemnity to the liturgy. But there were of course people who had the means of keeping a priest in their own household, and of exercising their authority to obtain one to look after their private chapel, often in a large and isolated country property. Thus we find private chaplains even in the early days of the Church. The councils protested, but they did so in vain. The custom had been introduced and accepted through the cupidity of certain prelates, and it was destined to have an interesting history.

After the Eleventh Century

So far we have gone no further than the eleventh century, and we have concentrated mainly on sixth and ninth century customs which are very important. In a brief essay such as this we cannot go into questions concerning the training of priests in those days, their way of life, their nomination, their emoluments (tithes for instance, introduced under Charlemagne) and the gradual development of their ministry. The outstanding fact that we have to note is that, in the eleventh century, there were town parishes and country parishes, the autonomy of the latter (the so-called baptismal or non-episcopal churches) becoming more and more the accepted thing. Whatever the title of the parish priest might be (pleban, or rector, or even *curio*) his office was stabilized. In the sixteenth century, the Council of Trent at its twenty-fourth session laid down a grave obligation on all parochi, or parish priests, to preach and instruct the faithful on all Sundays and holidays of obligation. Thus the parish priest was accepted definitively as the successor of the early bishops who had exclusive rights over preaching the Word.

Present-day canon law (can. 197) states that a parish priest enjoys "ordinary" powers, that is to say, he can even delegate some of his functions, except that of hearing confessions. He can absolve his own parishioners wherever they happen to be, and certain tasks are his by right, such as blessing the font, and assisting at marriages as the witness required by law. On holy Thursday he does not concelebrate with the bishop, but he celebrates Mass in his own church, with his own priests, to whom he gives communion before the faithful.

From the Beginning until the Present Day

If we compare the respective functions of bishops and priests, we can observe that they developed along opposite lines. The city priests of the first centuries were first and foremost assistants to the bishop at liturgical functions, at morning and evening prayer, baptisms, and Sunday Mass (which they concelebrated with him). They had no work of their own to do, because the deacons had sole charge of all welfare work. They did not preach because, for centuries, preaching was reserved to the bishop. They did not baptize, but only assisted the bishop at baptisms. They did not hear confessions, but assisted the bishop in the liturgical reconciliation of penitents. They did not solemnize marriages because the contracting parties in any case administer the sacrament to each other, and the Church had not by then laid down any canonical formula for marriage. They were not responsible for the children, because it was taken for granted that parents had to look after all their children's instruction in the faith, and it was the parents themselves who decided when the children should make their first communion. In fact the life of the priest was much more like that of monks to-day, apart from the fact that they visited the sick and kept close social ties with the people. Reforming bishops, like Eusebius of Vercelli or Saint Augustine of Hippo, were following a logical line of reasoning when they laid down a rule of life for their priests, including a regime of strict poverty. This movement for religious fervour went on throughout the Middle Ages, and was very much in favour in the eleventh and twelfth centuries. There was a flourishing tradition of abbot–bishops, especially in England, and the beautiful cloisters of French and English cathedrals indicate their monastic origins.

The story of the country priests, which we find from the sixth century onwards, is rather different. They seem to have been far more powerful than the priests in the towns, who were quite overshadowed by the bishop himself. Although the country priests were considered of second rank, they were, in their way, heads of churches.

They had their own deacons and clerics in minor orders, responsible for all the offices they could celebrate, and all the social and charitable work. They personally supervised the training of their own clergy, and even though they had no organized pastoral work or catechism, they were considered as persons of trust for everyone in the district, for the defence of the people's rights, and for help in temporal affairs. They were on an absolutely equal footing with the people among whom they lived, wore the same clothes as the people (except when they were celebrating the liturgy) had the same kind of culture and were perfectly familiar with the customs and trades of their flock. Despite all this, they were not envied by town priests, because it was considered such an honour to be with the bishop, particularly when, in the eighth and ninth centuries, he was a feudal lord.

Little by little, nearly all the pastoral functions of the early bishops were delegated to, or assumed by, the parish priests. To-day, in certain cases, they are able to administer the sacrament of confirmation, while every parish priest must be a missionary in some sense. The idea of the parish, as a "missionary community", is more than a mere formula, it is the sign of a general realization on the part of the clergy of the full magnitude of their task.

As the parish priests gradually took over the bishop's tasks, the bishop himself became less and less a pastor and more and more an administrator, reaching his flock only through his priests. This was inevitable if he wished to be free, not only to have easy access to his people, but also to his priests. From having been the head of *one* church, the bishop became, in fact, the head of all the church leaders in his diocese.

It could of course have happened otherwise. In the Christian East, even to-day, there are differences from country to country. In Italy there are two hundred dioceses and in pre-war Germany there were only twenty. The Merovingian kings had no wish to multiply bishops among the small towns and villages, because in their time the bishop was a temporal lord, and they did not wish to diminish him or bring dishonour on the episcopal rank. Had they done so, medieval Europe could have been like fourth-century Africa. What in any case stands out, is that neither parishes nor parish priests are of divine origin. They are an ecclesiastical institution.

History shows us, too, that the bishop's functions changed throughout the ages, and that nearly all of them were delegated to his subordinates, just as the original function of the apostles was, in the first century, divided into three – namely episcopate, priesthood and diaconate. Even though the terms "bishop" and "priest" were often synonymous and not even clearly defined, there is none the less a variation of first and second degree implied in the words.

Nowadays a priest's tasks are many and various. A priest is not only the liturgical representative of the people, preacher, head of the parish, or auxiliary head, and pastor of souls, he is also the children's catechist, spiritual director and guide. Sometimes he may be a school-teacher or educationalist responsible for various spiritual and temporal works, all necessary for that communion in charity which is implied by the union of the faithful that comes about through their participation in the Eucharist. Since, despite the express wish of the Council of Trent, we have no deacons to speak of, the priest has to do all these things. The priest has to be a teacher, a theologian, even something of a lawyer. Priests have the duty of forming the new clergy in the seminaries, and preparing them for their future work. No one priest could, nowadays, be responsible for teaching all that the seminarian has to master in the way of dogma, moral theology, philosophy, exegesis, canon law, psychology, pastoral theology and liturgy, church history, etc. A priest has to be an educated man, with a knowledge of philosophy, able to defend the faith in matters of philosophy and science. One priest alone cannot take on himself all the priestly functions. These are to be found solely in the unique priesthood of the bishop, who, in the last instance, is responsible for seeing that they are carried out.

Conclusion

The office of parish priest has, in common with all his other ministrations, arisen through a differentiation of the episcopal function. It evolved slowly between the fourth and ninth centuries. Not until the eleventh century is it possible to identify him with the parish priest of to-day, and we certainly cannot claim that the parish priest has ceased to evolve, any more than we can say that a bishop's commitments are limited to those which we recognize as his to-day. Priests and bishops alike are, after all, responsible for certain holy and spiritual things which cannot be clearly defined, which are not dead but, on the contrary, very much alive, still developing and maturing so that they always need to be adapted to contemporary needs. Living things have precisely that quality of being able to adapt themselves without changing their nature. The faith, the sacraments, are real things. It is these that dictate what the functions of a priest should be in any particular period of the church's history. They likewise define what changes and developments must take place in all that is not of divine origin in the Church.

In the Middle Ages, the Church showed herself capable of using imagination and courage when she had to give to the hitherto neglected rural areas a type of church which would fulfil their requirements. That is how parish organization began. To-day, no less than formerly, imagination and courage are still necessary if we are to adapt the Church to the different social strata, the differing levels of living that we find in modern society. For the boundaries of Christendom in our time are no longer the rural areas surrounding the bishop's church. They are the boundaries that define social classes and social sectors. The pagans of to-day are not necessarily inhabitants of the *pagi*. They have no special habitat. They are with us everywhere.

Chapter Three

WHERE DO THEY COME FROM?

His clerical dress, the vow depriving him of wife and child, his whole education and outlook, all tend to make a priest something out of this world. One would gather, from the way in which some people treat him, that he can hardly be made of flesh and blood. It is as well to remember then, that every priest was a child once, that he grew up like other children, and that during his early days, at least, he was quite indistinguishable from all the others.

Some people find it difficult to imagine what it must be like to have a child growing up in the family, who has the idea of becoming a priest some day. Yet it is happening in many families, at every level of society, all the time. The Church must be unique in that it draws its ministers from all walks of life and excludes absolutely none. St. Pius X used to go to school barefoot, carrying his shoes slung over his shoulder to make them last longer. Pius XII was born a Roman nobleman. In any seminary you will find boys from poor families studying together with the sons of the wealthy, and being quite unconcerned about it. Admittedly, at certain times in the Church's history one finds more vocations coming from one particular class of society, but it would be quite impossible to draw any conclusions that would apply to the Church as a whole.

Vocations arise where the Spirit wills whatever people may say to the contrary. You will often hear such speculations as: "Going to be a priest at twenty? Must have been jilted by his girl friend . . .!" or "Can you see that child being a priest? Ridiculous! Obviously it's his mother idea . . . ." But whatever people may think, or say, a few years in a seminary will discover whether or not this or that child, or youth, or late vocation, is really called by God.

Age is as irrelevant as social standing. One can be admitted to a junior seminary to continue one's education before beginning priestly studies, or one can go to a seminary on leaving school. Others begin at the age of twenty-five, thirty, forty even later. Late vocations have never been more numerous than at the present day, and they are invaluable to the modern Church and her problems. The advantages of having come into contact with the realities of life, of having already followed some trade or profession, are obvious enough when the contemporary task is to put the Church right in the centre of a pagan and materialistic world, where she is most needed.

In one seminary I knew a student who wore two wedding rings on his finger – his own, and his wife's. She died two years after they were married. But one would be very

41

wrong to suppose that his decision to become a priest was prompted by grief or the search for some kind of consolation. The truth was that God had used the foregoing years, their engagement and brief married life together, as a preparation for his vocation. These preparatory years are no rare thing either. Quite often one finds a widower taking up the priesthood after one or two of his sons have been ordained.

Some vocations are even more mysterious, and not all of them achieve the publicity of, for instance, Psichari, the grandson of Renan, the famous atheist. With him there was the overpowering sense of a need to go back to the faith of his forefathers. It came suddenly, out in the desert, as a call that could not be denied. One of the less known, but no less startling cases, came to my notice in a district that was very much divided between clericals and anti-clericals. Things had reached such a pitch that there had to be two doctors, two lawyers, two chemists, even two bakers, to supply the needs of the two groups that could not tolerate each other! One day, without any warning, the grandson of the anti-clerical doctor (who more or less led his faction) told his grandfather that he was going to be a priest. One can hardly suggest, in his case, that his family were coercing him into holy orders.

In some religions, the priesthood belongs to one caste, to one exclusive portion of society. In the Catholic Church,

simply on account of celibacy, there is no possibility of
the priesthood being handed on in the same families for
generation after generation. This means a constant renewal
within the ranks of the priesthood. Its ministers can
be the sons of bakers, or professors, or farm labourers, or
justices of the peace, and consequently there is a constantly renewed stream of vitality flowing into the
priesthood.

If a priest really is Christ living among the people, his
name and family are of the least importance. There is no
calling in which the family background matters less. The
thing that matters vitally is the person of the priest himself,
because his Christ-likeness is going to be inestimably
increased if he is spiritually developed, if his education
has really trained his mind, and if he has personality,
understanding, and commonsense.

In some walks of life, upbringing has no influence on
one's work. Two manual workers may produce identical
things, and if one has been brought up in an orphanage,
and the other by his own parents, it makes no difference.
The same is true for a businessman, or an official. But for
those whose work concerns people, psychological factors
are obviously more important. Doctors, social workers,
teachers, need first and foremost a good brain. Without
it, the very best human qualities will not equip them for
their jobs. For a priest, particularly in the world of to-day,

the greatest possible acquisition is a sensitivity with regard to other people. He must be well educated, he must know his theology, canon law and the rest. But education is not enough for a priest. He will be a sorry pastor who can offer his people nothing but brains.

In a parish where the majority practise their religion, people will no doubt be satisfied with a priest who does his pastoral work in the way it should be done, and ask nothing more of him. He is their intermediary with God, and that is, strictly speaking, all they need. But supposing he can offer them, together with his due service, a personality which is full and rich, a spirit which is alive, and ready to meet the needs of each one of them? Obviously the whole parish will be the better off for having him. If he is an attractive personality, someone full of ideas and the capacity to stimulate interest, someone active and enterprising, his parish will in time become a faithful mirror of its spiritual leader. He will communicate to everyone his own life and enthusiasm.

If the parish is one where people have either drifted away from the faith or never really been in possession of it, a priest's human qualities are even more valuable. People will not give him their confidence, so he must learn to read their secrets in other ways. He must find the pulse intuitively. To make contact with people who are spiritually far removed from religion, he must bridge the gap between them and God by means of his willingness to see things from their angle, to make advances, and show himself a ready listener when they are prepared to talk; to judge shrewdly, and to be infinitely patient. These are human qualities, and they are indispensable.

Over and above the things which every priest has to do in any parish, there is still a great deal of scope for the particular kind of parish activity to which his own zeal and initiative and interest incline him. It is quite to be expected that there is something in the life of every priest which, because of his temperament, he considers particularly worth-while in connection with the work of saving people's souls. When a new parish priest arrives, the people are immediately on the lookout, whether consciously or not, for the particular line he will take. They know that they will be asked for some sort of participation in the approach he adopts. His preferences, his ideas, his outlook, are all going to leave their mark on the parish for good or ill.

Even a quick and superficial observation can tell them what sort of man the new priest is. Priests do in fact conform to a series of types, with which we are all familiar. We immediately recognize the priest whom pious people will readily think a "mystic", because his mind is so clearly intent on prayer and the things of God. In France, he is the sort that one finds most often in church. He has a fondness for God's house and God's service, with all the ceremony that this entails. He is insistent on his people frequenting the sacraments, and being regular in their prayers, and he is always ready to talk to them about the interior life as soon as they show any taste for it.

Then there is the liturgist, who has an even more developed taste for ceremonial. He is scrupulous about the least little rubric, and his aim is to get together a really magnificent choir, and to produce a perfect turn-out on every solemn occasion. The glory of God is seen almost exclusively in terms of plain-chant exquisitely rendered.

As an antithesis to these two you will find a class of active and enterprising priests. These are the builders, who can never stop adding to the church, or renovating it, or putting up bigger and better parish halls and schools. Their schemes are inevitably a trifle exhausting on parishioners' pockets, and Sunday sermons tend to be mere variations of the great building theme. Then there are the administrative priests, whose accounts are always in wonderful order, and whom one tends to picture in front of a typewriter, surrounded by files, with the telephone in easy reach. They always know exactly how much each collection brought in, precisely what the parish debts are, and what the parish income is. Their chief grouse is the lamentable state the books were in when they came; their great boast that whoever takes over from them will have everything under perfect control. And this means not only the accounts, but the parishioners too! Each family has its own card in the card index system, each factory with its significant label, red blue or green! What more could you want?

Then there is the organizer, who seems to feel that the universal Church is bigger and richer and safer if he can add to the number of her groups and meetings and societies for this and that. He likes to run things, and preside and order people about – in the nicest possible way of course.

I remember reading an article in *La Croix,* written many years ago by Pierre l'Ermite, who visualized all the different sort of priests going to heaven. Each one explained to Saint Peter what he had done during his lifetime. The first had been a teacher, and explained with modest pride how he had sacrificed himself for his pupils, and done everything he could to improve his mind. Saint Peter was not impressed but let him in none the less.

The second had specialized in the spiritual direction of women. "They should have sent you to the garden of Eden", Saint Peter said, "still, never mind – come on in . . . ."

The third had been a great preacher. He had preached literally everywhere. And he had preached nothing but the gospel. Saint Peter began to look pleased.

The next priest had devoted his life to the children's

catechism, "trying to make it *live* for them", as he explained. Better and better, thought Saint Peter!

I forget how many more candidates there were, but the last one of all, I do remember. His cassock was in rather a mess, and he was neither well groomed nor particularly well shaven. He was full of thoughts that had nothing to do with going to heaven. Obviously a busy man, with no time for anything extra like that. "Well, and what did you do?" Saint Peter asked. "Nothing special", was the weary answer. "I just did what I could for people." Saint Peter echoed the answer with pleasure, and led him in person to the seventh heaven.

The priesthood might, in fact, be compared to an enormous keyboard instrument, on which every priest plays according to the particular talent he possesses. And of course the inspiration of his playing goes back to his early days, the impressionable years of childhood and youth, which helped to make him the priest he is now.

As soon as a child conceives the ambition of becoming a priest, the future Father X. is already there, in embryo. The finished portrait is made up of family background, home, circumstances, every impression he was capable of receiving in his youth. Perhaps as a child he was of a gentle disposition, and easily taught. No doubt his mother played her part there, her permanent mark in his character being those qualities of infinite value – tact and delicacy.

On the other hand, mamma can leave less pleasant marks – a suspiciously feminine taste for lace albs and lavish vestments, or a thirst for precedence! Take another child, this time one who has known hardship, but managed to thrive on it, and is full of energy and mischief. He is unlikely to become a contemplative type but no one is going to hold that against him.

Circumstances, too, are important, and the people he meets and who influence him, and the things that may change the course of his whole life – his military service, for instance, an illness, or some family crisis. The individual is affected by all this, and so, later on, is the parish, through this particular priest. Fortunately the seminary cannot be held exclusively responsible for the formation of our priests, because if this were the case, they would be very stereotyped.

If you are surprised by the outlook, and even the language of some priests, it *can* be the result of their having been brought up in a seminary from an early age. But do not hold this against them. The abbé Godin was just such a typical little seminarian, timid, sickly, scrupulous – yet he became one of the most realistic and wide-awake priests our century has known. Canon Cardijn promised his dying father that he would dedicate his life to the salvation of the workers, and that promise has been brilliantly realized. There are many vocations that germi-

49

nated in factories, which now are among the Church's finest apostles.

Of course you will find priests who come from the humblest background, who have been only too happy to break with the humiliations of their childhood. I know one who wears an astrakhan collar on his coat, and has quite given up any thought of working among the poor. His hunting ground now is the smart salon. His mother sold vegetables. But thank God we also find priests who were brought up in comfort and refinement, devoting themselves utterly to the workers and peasants. I know one among the worker-priests who is the son of a big industrialist.

It is not only a priest's home and family background that make their mark on him. As he goes on in the ministry, the environment in which he works will also influence him, together with all the satisfaction he gets out of serving others, all the disappointments he has to accept, and all the burdens he must bear. A priest who is new in the ministry will also come very much under the influence of the parish rector, who is responsible in some degree for his formation. Circumstances, too, are very important, for they may change a priest's tastes altogether. Someone who had always seen himself settling down in some quiet country place, is amazed to discover, on being sent to some busy suburb, an unsuspected inclination and aptitude for the popular apostolate.

A great deal of very valuable influence could come from the parishioners themselves, but unfortunately priests are often quite unaware of what their parishioners really think of them. They hear their priest in the pulpit every Sunday, they see the way he reacts to the various problems that occur in connection with themselves and local government officials, but so often they forget that it would be an act of fraternal charity to tell him what they think of the way he conducts affairs. They could often give him valuable advice, which would be a service not only to him but to the Church herself. They rarely seem to realize that they, as well as the priest, *are* the parish, and that he often needs their guidance. Sometimes he needs to be warned, even contradicted and opposed.

The sad thing is that, far from hearing the truth about himself from their lips, a priest is often deluded by what are deliberate lies. If he is a bad preacher for instance, it is much more constructive to tell him so, and not to praise him for good sermons until he is able to give a good one. He may not have bothered to familiarize himself with the special problems of his locality. He may have caused unnecessary disturbance, in which case it is thoroughly wrong for people to congratulate him on getting along so well in the parish. Priests can have their heads turned with false compliments, they can be spoiled by being showered with presents, by too much sympathy, or by undue servility.

By all means honour the priesthood, but have a care for the man who bears it. In seeking to honour him you may dishonour the priesthood.

It may seem a contradiction, at this stage, to affirm that the only really important thing for a priest is his priesthood, despite whatever good qualities he may have as a result of his home background and his culture. But the fact remains that whatever good qualities he may possess as a man, these are merely instruments. They will help him to do wonderful work, but they are instruments all the same. He will be a good priest, first and foremost, if he puts his whole person at the service of his priesthood. There are two ways open to him for developing his personal gifts. He can consider them as his sole stock in trade, and build his whole apostolic activity around them, or he can accept them simply and humbly as a gift from God and dedicate them to his priestly work, using them as instruments with which he unceasingly bestows and fulfils himself.

"Mediocre men make the best priests", I was told by my first parish priest. He had in mind, he assured me, someone who was by no means gifted, but who had an enormous success as a parish priest. He meant, by "mediocre men", those who do not put their personal qualities to the fore, using them as stepping stones to pre-eminence, or wearing them like an aura of success. He meant the sort of preacher who makes no effort to shine, or impress or carry his audience away by eloquence alone. He meant the sort of priest who does not depend on himself for the success of his work, but prefers to allow grace to work through him – the grace of Christ in the priesthood, which Christ himself has put at his disposal.

If a priest is willing to submit himself to the fact that the priesthood comes first in his life, he becomes acutely sensitive to this great reality when he has faced it. It will transform his whole priestly life. We have a wonderful example of this in Cardinal Suhard. There is no need to conceal the fact that his election as archbishop of Paris was not welcomed by everyone. He was used to the apostolate in rural areas, where he had been very much concerned in curial affairs. Few people thought of him as the obvious choice for Paris, or indeed for any other place where modern problems demand that the apostolate be thought out in terms of a particular, and peculiar situation. These people forgot, however, that Suhard was a priest first and last, and that he was if anything hypersensitive to the demands which his priesthood made of him. And so it was not so very surprising, after all, to see him revealed as one of the greatest apostles of our time, certainly the most enterprising, intuitive and daring pastor that Paris has ever had.

Finally, I feel I must take back a little of what I said about the different types of priest at the beginning of this chapter. Humanity is infinitely varied, and there are all sorts and conditions of men looking after our parishes, of every shade of character and outlook. Fundamental to them all, however, in one degree or another, you will find the common factor which stereotypes them all, and that is the thirst for souls. The basic type of priest is – the apostle.

Chapter Four

THE PASTOR

THE man in the street finds no difficulty in telling you what a parish priest's job is. He looks after a church – the one he is given to look after. He looks after it, beautifies it possibly, adds to it, or even rebuilds it if it is falling to pieces, or is not big enough. He has fine ceremonies in the church, and these would appear to be his principal occupation in life. "The parish priest is a very happy man", I was told by someone who in fact knew little about what he was saying. "He has everything he wants, – statues, vestments, pictures – simply by asking for them from the pulpit!"

Yes, at first glance it might seem as if a parish priest had only to see that the church services were nicely carried out, and that the children got their catechism. Then, depending on his energy, he may visit the sick. Depending on his charity he may give some relief to the poor.

But those who are really acquainted with their priest know that, to-day at least, there are new needs to be faced. There are so many people who will not attend church and we have to try to persuade them to come. So many children are brought up without any religion, without any moral sense or even any idea of normal conventions. A priest has to see to all this, organizing centres and clubs, and it is a refreshing change when someone realizes that he is not doing it just for his own amusement. When I was a curate in a provincial parish, I went to find out why a certain youth had stopped coming to the *patronage** on Thursday afternoons. "He'll come all right, Father," his mother told me, and continued, "I quite understand that a young priest like you needs something to help pass the time". Obviously, she thought I looked forward to my Thursdays for a chance to play with the children. This situation has become so generally accepted that some parents get quite annoyed with the priest if he fails to take their children off their hands on Thursday and Sunday afternoons!

Young people and children have to be encouraged to take an interest in their faith. It must be made attractive for them. That is why priests organize clubs where they can have sports, and music and study circles. For the grown-ups, the parish clergy organize cinema shows and theatricals. So that nowadays, what with one thing and another, the parish priest really *has* got something to do. Some of his parishioners feel sorry for him – others are glad to see that he is busy. "What else would he have to do", they ask, "in a parish where not many people go to

---

* A catechism class and youth club.

church anyway? He can't spend his whole day on a handful of old women." They are not surprised, therefore, to see him take up a few new occupations.

Having realized, however, that he is doing these things, have people really come to an understanding of the priest's real mission in life? Do they ask whether these activities are the principal ones, or mere adjuncts, means for getting at ends, one or two useful little jobs to help him achieve the essential? The part that people see, the concrete side of his work, is only one facet, and it can be completely misleading.

The priest's job is to look after the Church, we are agreed, but the Church is something living. His parish is, or should be part of the living Church. He is pastor of his flock, and his flock does not consist of sheep asleep, or of dead mutton. The flock is on the move, and he is responsible for the direction it takes. He is responsible for the food it gets, by which we mean the gospel. And this being the case, his task can never come to an end.

I remember one of my friends at school, who gave up his studies and took a job instead. He became a grocer's assistant. Every evening, at about seven o'clock, I would see him tidying up the shop. We would exchange a few words, and he would say "All over for to-day!" I used to feel sorry for myself, with all those books in my satchel – mathematics, history, literature, – and the prospect of an evening spent on exercises, compositions, translations. How I envied him, and how I longed to have a job that I could stop at the end of the day, knowing that I could say "That's finished".

Now, after all the years that I have spent in the priesthood, I always have to say, at the end of each day, "I've hardly begun . . .", because, of course, a priest's life cannot be neatly rounded off like that of most business and professional men. A priest's work is always in process of getting somewhere, and is never finished. Each new effort he makes shows him how much more he still has to do. Each new activity that he starts opens further vistas for more activity. Every little progress only helps him to see something more that has to be achieved.

Because, after all, the parish priest has to think of all the children when it comes to seeing that they grow up in the light of Christ – not just the ones who go to his school and come to the *patronage,* but all the children in his parish. He cannot be satisfied or secure in the mere knowledge that the children are at least housed within the walls that he, or his predecessors, built. He knows that the utmost must be done to ensure that all possible benefit may be gained for them. As long as there is some child unaccounted for, he cannot but think of the parable of the ninety-nine, and the one which was lost and found again by the Good Shepherd. Those who are furthest removed from his care are precisely the ones who must cause a priest the most concern, and inevitably the most pain.

But even the question of the children is by no means the first thing on a priest's agenda. What would be the good of looking after the children if their adolescence were later neglected? They have to be followed up, and the light which they saw as children must be there at the age when they begin to have ideals, altruisms. It is then that they absolutely must have Christ with them, to share in his strength and his greatness.

The young people have to be taught, and given good habits of Christian living. They need inspiration, they have to have enthusiasm instilled into them, so that when they marry, the homes that they start will have the same ideal that they themselves were given. Young couples are a priest's responsibility. He has to answer for what goes on in these young families. It is he who must show young parents, as they become more aware of life opening out before them, how love can deepen its motivating force if it burns with the charity of Jesus.

There is not a single home or family in the parish for which the priest can disclaim responsibility. Not that he has to shoulder all their cares for them, and certainly not that he has the right to meddle in their affairs. It is his responsibility to see that the life of the spirit flourishes within families, and that all the hard things in life, our passions and our selfishness, do not prevent souls from coming to Christ. Not only *sub specie aeternitatis,* but in the practical human circumstances of every day life, the shepherd must be always thinking about his sheep. If he loves them, their problems will be his, because our Lord gave them to him. Their sufferings are his sufferings. All these people need the gospel as a light on their daily path, whether as individuals who have to answer for their own salvation, or as mothers and fathers, employers and employees, responsible also for the salvation of others. No one is going to enlighten all these people about the demands of God's will in their lives, unless it be the parish priest. No one else will shoulder their responsibilities, or help them to shoulder those of their dependants. No one else will be there to guide them with his instruction, or help them with his encouragement.

A parish priest has to extend his care to everyone, including the old man who sits in the sun to warm his weary bones for one more day, or dies in some forgotten corner. The priest is responsible for their last hours, as well as their early days. One is as important as the other. He must be there from the beginning to the end, from the first stage of the catechism to the last minutes in which he can see to it that eternity shines through the consolations which the Church offers, and through the final act of hope.

Whatever he may think about it, the parish priest will have to answer for them all, and those who take the most trouble to avoid him are the ones he must consider as his biggest responsibility. The first thing that the Curé d'Ars did on arriving at his parish with his few little possessions, was to fall on his knees in prayer at the thought of the burden he was about to take up. Whenever a priest takes over a new district, he looks about him and says (or should say) to himself "All these people are my concern". Wherever he meets his parishioners, even though they deliberately ignore him, they are as near to him, without realizing it, as children are to their father, or disciples to their master. However hostile they may be, however poorly situated, however morally disorganized or even completely indifferent to religion – they are his business. If they are not, then he is not a pastor at all – not a shepherd but only a hireling: "someone who does it for the money".

What are his exact responsibilities regarding all these people? First of all, obviously, to answer the Master's call to "Go, teach the gospel to every creature . . . baptize them in God, in the Father, the Son and the Spirit".

It is primarily a preaching mission. He has to talk about Christ to the people who have never heard of him. He has to reveal Christ more deeply to those who already believe they know him. He must preach, at no matter what cost to himself, whether in public or in private, in church or in people's homes. He has to find a way into people's minds and hearts. He has to know how to talk to the people in twentieth-century (and not eighteenth-century) language. However hard the way may be, a priest *must* preach the gospel. It is better to be direct than not. There is no point in pretending that there are times when we had better keep silence, as if to allow the secret germination of some seed which heaven knows who has planted. That is not Saint Paul's way, and it is not the Church's way either. Nor do a priest's responsibilities end with the individuals themselves. People form themselves into groups, and parties of all kinds, so that he has to keep an eye on these too. If it is true to say that people deserve the government they get, it is equally true to say that all human institutions are what men make them. An institution can help us to develop, or it can suffocate us entirely. It all depends on the amount of enlightenment, liberty and scope that is offered in our organizations. We find often enough that one generation seems to be living entirely on the ideas and conventions of its grandfathers. These may still be a source of inspiration, but they are more likely to be a source of atrophy. We always have to be sufficiently well nourished in the spiritual sphere

62

to have the strength to overcome the restrictions that the past tends to lay upon us.

For a Christian, no particular established order can ever be synonymous with "order" as an abstract value. Others may, and do, identify the background and ideals with which they have grown up and prospered, with the eternal moral order. But the Christian knows that every order is capable of being improved, and that every society is capable of advancing. No particular age can possibly bring about, on this earth, a state of affairs that is so perfect that it could last for ever.

It is important for the parish priest to remember this. He is familiar with all the wretchedness that, more often than not, is pushed out of sight in modern society. His task is to bring it to light, to expose it, to bring it to the notice of those more fortunate, whose selfishness is responsible for the fact that the really needy are elbowed into society's dark corners.

He knows the slums, for instance, places where souls as well as bodies are prostituted. He cannot go down these streets without suffering, and without an intense desire that this should all be changed. He knows the big blocks where several hundred families are all crowded together and he knows the dangers of living in such close contact. Something, he says, has got to be done about it. Then there are the factories, two or three in his parish perhaps, where a couple of thousand of his parishioners spend their day, and come out each evening worn out, utterly jaded, incapable of making any effort to turn what is left of their day into something profitable for the mind or the soul. These are places where, as Pius XI said, "raw material is refined, and human beings are degraded . . .". All this is a heavy weight on any priest's mind, if he accepts his responsibility, knowing that something absolutely *must* be done to change what is wrong.

In the evening, as he turns down certain streets, passes certain doors and cafés, he sees women standing – waiting. These too are his parishioners, purveyors of sin, some of them willing, some forced by circumstance. This, he says, cannot continue. He knows which are the cinemas and public places where the young people can find sin easily, where they are spoiled, embittered – where they putrefy, literally. Something must be done, for them, just as conditions must change for every starving child, every woman in rags. All day long he can hear the worries of mothers who have not got enough money, of young people who want to get married and cannot find a place to live, out of work labourers, and plenty more who work, but are exploited by their employers. And so the "established order" is bound to fill him with anxiety, just as it fills him with the sufferings of those who come to him for sympathy. His mind eventually becomes fixed on one point, a future that must be, O God, *must be* better than this!

He admits that, as Christ's envoy, he is bound to "render to Caesar the things which are Caesar's, and to God what is God's", and that his mission is to preach a kingdom that is not of this world. But it is equally true that "to practise virtue one must have at least the minimum of physical well-being", as Leo XIII said. A parish priest knows, through his own experience, and not merely in theory, that wages are often inadequate, that housing is often non-existent, and that the factories are often thoroughly bad. He knows this because he knows his parishioners and their difficulties and their misery. Whenever he thinks of conditions in his parish he does so in terms of faces whose sorrow he shares, and names of people with whom he suffers.

And so he cannot wait until things have changed for the better before preaching the kingdom of God. Saint Paul did not wait for the Roman world to abolish slavery before he spoke about Christ, because it is precisely by putting Christ in people's hearts that human society changes. At the same time, however, a parish priest's job is not to change the social order. He has no right to re-design society according to his own lights or his own preferences.

In past ages, the Church has realized some remarkable

social achievements, beginning with the monks who started by cultivating virgin land, building hospitals, founding schools and so on. Even to-day, in some primitive countries, missionaries may have to undertake certain projects that the faithful could not manage without their help, and which serve as an example to be followed. But in a society that is already highly developed, the clergy cannot treat the laity as if they were children. The laity themselves have to take a major part. A priest nowadays is not responsible for undertaking new social organizations, or even getting others to undertake them. What he has to do is to see to it that all those under his care are able to realize what are the demands that the gospel makes of each member and of the whole community. If he can do this, then the laymen themselves can take all the necessary steps, and bring about all the necessary changes.

Priests must always be on their guard against clericalism. One could even go so far as to say that of all the people in the parish, the parish priest himself should be the "anticlerical" *par excellence*. Clericalism, in his case, means imposing his own views, his own conception of true order, and forgetting that the laymen themselves, not the priest, are to put everything into practice.

Priests must not forget that although the clergy and the laity are two complementary entities in the Church, in society they act on two totally different levels. The layman has his own responsibilities. Even if the priest is a perfect organizer, even if he is capable of bringing about all the necessary changes himself through his own talents, still he could never say that it was his duty to put himself at the head of a movement for social reform. His duty is to preach, and to educate the faithful in their Christian duty. His aim should not be to "get there more quickly", but to make every Christian realize what is required of him.

When we speak of laymen we do not mean only those who are willing to group themselves around their pastor and come to him for their inspiration, and accept what he has to tell them. "Layman" means everyman – all people in this world, because Christ should enlighten them all.

The Church has certainly changed her attitude through the ages. In the middle ages, for instance, the faithful lived "inside" Christianity, as within a strongly walled castle, protected against the Moors, Saracens and others who might threaten from without. But in our time, faithful and pagans are all mixed up together, sharing the same human obligations, and directing one and the same society on equal terms. This is obviously a good thing, because it means that the Church has become what Our Lord wanted her to be: the leaven in the lump . . . the salt that gives savour to everything into which it is put.

But granted that we have had the good fortune to find

our way back into the Church of our Lord's own conception, we have to be sure that we are being a real leaven. Why is yeast put into bread, if not to raise up, by its own strength, what would otherwise remain a lump of dough? The whole point of putting salt into our food is to give it a flavour, and if the salt has lost this power to put the flavour in food, what can we use instead? A priest's duties are endless, because the gospel has to reach into the farthest corner of his parish, just like the circulation of blood taking life into every part of the human body.

Christianity in our time is not something separate, it is clearly bound up with the everyday world. Leavening the lump, its function is to make the whole of society into a unity. Christ's last prayer was that we might be one. A Christian cannot really live alone. He is essentially a member of a community. One has the impression that the Holy Spirit can only influence the world in and through communities. In the first place, he came down on the apostles when they were all gathered together in the upper room. The religion of Christ was spread far and wide by the witness of the early Christian communities, when it could be said of them that they had "one heart and one soul". Christianity to-day, as yesterday, is stronger than any paganism and any persecution, but it can only spread by means of strong groups, everywhere. No parish can be saved merely by one or two people doing one or two pious things. Its mission can only be fulfilled if it has, at its very centre, a living nucleus of real Christians, who are true brothers among themselves, and a burning and shining light to those about them.

This is not to say that the apostolate of any one individual is to be minimized, but obviously the greater light will be shed when a parish ceases to be a ghetto for practising Catholics, and it becomes plain for all to see that here are Christians who are happy in the faith they profess, and happy because they are united to Christ, and to each other, through charity.

A parish priest could, in fact, be defined as one who wakes up community consciousness, and builds communities. In the first place it is the young people who need to be formed into some sort of group, in which they may realize all together what has to be done if the future is to be saved. Within the group, their enthusiasm can be communicated from one to another, and their ambitions and ideals defined in the general interchange of friendship. Then when the young ones grow up, wherever they may happen to live, they must know each other as Christians, and love and help one another for the rest of their lives. I met a man from a suburban parish who told me that something had changed while he was away at the war. He could not put his finger, he said, on the precise nature of the change. His neighbours were the same, things went on in the same way, and yet everything seemed different. A few weeks later he realized what had happened. "As far as I can see", he said, "the difference is in the people who used to go to Mass every Sunday without getting to know each other. Now they do know one another, and they get on so well together that the whole place has completely changed." The same thing happened in a large tenement, when the practising Catholics were encouraged to get together. "We really didn't know each other at all", they said, "we weren't even sure who went to Mass and who didn't". Two old people, turning to a young couple, confessed, "We always used to think it was you who pushed those terrible anti-Catholic pamphlets under our door". Now it was all different. They all knew one another; the tenement was a new place. They were all friends, helping another. That is only one aspect of the mission which should be undertaken in every parish where the priest is conscious of his duty.

We have to wake up people to the realization that we are meant to live as Christians in community. It is the priest who has to bring the community into being, in every walk of society. It is not just a question of getting working people together to realize that work is something good and noble, and to discuss how they can face up to certain problems in connection with their rights and their duties. They have to learn that they are always meant to help each other, the whole way through life. Together, in groups of infinitely varied proportion, they can pass on the gospel to those around them. Christ's charity must radiate into every corner of society, not only in words, but in "action and truth". The parish priest's task is to bring into being such a community consciousness that all Christians, whatever their social standing, can see that their salvation, and that of their fellow men, is bound up in the group.

It is a big job for a pastor. It is not easy to make everyone conscious of his duty. A priest needs a great deal of the spirit of self-sacrifice if he is to put up with people's slowness and witlessness, and never stop drumming into them the fact that urgent and necessary things must be done, *now*! He has to be a brave man too, to go on goading people mercilessly to realize what God demands of them.

In a rather pagan country parish, the new priest was greeted by one lady (whose intention was simply to sing the praises of his predecessor) with, "Father X. was *such* a nice man! He never used to tell us off". What would she say about me, he wondered, if I started telling her off?

A parish priest often has to be unpleasant if he is eager to preach truth and justice. It would be a very odd thing if he never had to say anything unpleasant to anyone. It could only mean that he was either too blind or too timid to do so. During a strike, for instance, a priest has

71

often to take sides, like anyone else. He is not called upon to arbitrate but he is bound to have an opinion. His work can often be very difficult, his position awkward, if he wants to live up to the demands of the gospel and yet not interfere. Take the case, for example, of a country parish where there is a high level of churchgoing, and the farm labourers (never very highly paid) get together and decide that none of them will accept less than a certain minimum. Then the farmers meet together and decide to take the whole matter to the priest for his decision. The parish is dependent on the farmers for financial support. Still he is asked to state publicly what is the Christian thing to do – in a community where people are in fact practising Christians. The priest certainly has a duty, however unpleasant it may be to perform.

All this is but an outline of the parish priest's commitments. There is a host of other things to see to. This is no more a definition of a priest's work than, let us say, housework, cooking and mending defines the duty of a housewife. Something new is always arising, and his work, like hers, is never done.

Take the case of an old country priest. Most people would suppose that he had very little to do, but the fact remains that all his parishioners depend on him. He may not have very many practising Catholics to look after, but they are sure to be spread over a large area, which means that both he and they have to cover distances to get to each other. If we minimize his work by saying that he has to look after only a few people, we are immediately pointing out what a great deal still remains to be done.

Then there is the priest whose parishioners are so good that they nearly all go to Mass, everyone from the mayor downwards being the sort of people who at least claim to lead Christian lives. Does this mean that he can sit at home waiting for the bell to be rung by people requesting him to take the sacraments to the sick and the dying? Obviously not, if his parishioners really are listening to what he tells them from the pulpit, and want to be real Christians, modelling their lives on the gospel. Even if these people are only attached to their faith because it is a safe anchorage in a troubled world, a means of making legitimate an accepted social order that safeguards their interests and their privileges, this only implies further responsibilities for the priest, because he still has to inform them what their real duty as Christians is. If they really want their country to be Christian, it must be a true witness to the gospel and not a caricature.

The parish priest must always be on the look-out for possible deviations from the gospel. If his people listen to him he has all the more encouragement for pointing out their mistakes, their selfishness, the prejudices and preconceptions that are not in conformity with the will of

Christ. It would be very wrong to leave any parish that considers itself Christian to its own devices. This way lies the hardening of its arteries, pharisaism and conventionality.

If a parish is really Christian, it has a mission to communicate to other parishes, other people, the spiritual riches it implies its members possess, and others may lack. The parish priest cannot go to sleep, lulled by the rhythm of well ordered lives full of consoling fervour. His job is obviously to point out the misery that may well lie just over his boundary, and to form apostles and missionaries among his people to go and deal with it.

Then we have the town parishes, where one pastor is responsible for thousands of souls. How on earth can he get to know and cope with them all? He can never really get to grips with all the reasons why they fall away from the faith. He will always be submerged by his work. He will always feel crushed by the sheer number of his obligations to his people.

No, a parish priest who realizes what his commitment is never comes to the end of his work. That is, of course, if he is a real parish priest – a pastor, and not a mere hireling.

Chapter Five

A PRIEST'S WORK

THERE is a certain type of office worker and local government official whom we feel we cannot praise more highly when we say how conscientious he is, how punctual, how hard-working and reliable. This is a compliment, because it means that during his office hours he is putting in the maximum effort.

If we thought that this were the sort of compliment one could pay to a priest, it would presumably mean that we approved of those priests who say, "I'm afraid you've come at the wrong time", or "You can't expect me to do this to-day", or "That is nothing to do with me". The truth is, however, that most of us are very put off by the priest who is so imbued with the administrative outlook, that we have the impression of being received by a civil servant as soon as the presbytery door is opened to us. We cannot see how a priest can be a slave to his timetable, his immediate commitments and rubber stamps. He may have canon law on his side, and the express wishes of his superiors do not require him to do more than he does, but the truth is that his obligations as a pastor cannot be neatly laid down in black and white.

A real pastoral priest is not satisfied with telling everyone just exactly what his job entails, and then refusing to go outside its clearly defined limits. This is because all the jobs he has to do, no matter how holy they are, are still only means to an end. They are not ends in themselves. The ends that he aims at are not immediate, they are out of this world. His main care is not to exercise a profession, or fill up his life with useful activity. It is to add to all the good that is being done in the world.

Whereas some priests are called to specific tasks such as education, preaching, spiritual direction, or Catholic Action, a parish priest has to cope with all these things. In France, as soon as he takes over a parish, the bishop's delegate conducts him publicly round the church, handing over to his care everything in it – the tabernacle, the door keys, the church bells, the font, the confessional, the pulpit, and finally the sanctuary itself. This significant little ceremony symbolizes the variety of work he is called upon, as a parish priest, to undertake, and carry out to the full.

The church that he has been given to look after is the house of God's people. It is his duty to call them to church, although in these modern times, it is only in country districts that one finds the parish priest ringing the bells himself. Electricity has taken a hand in many town belfries! He has to call them to church, but in a pleasant way, not with threats, nor in terms of obligation. It is his business to make the church, and all that goes on in it, attractive to his people. It should welcome them. They must want to *like* coming to church. It is here that they must come for the food of their souls, which means a spiritual recreation, a getting together with each other. At church services they should be having a "good time", literally. They must all feel at home here, and at their ease. University graduates and factory workers must feel equally that they are in their father's house. There must be nothing there to get on the nerves of either of them, nothing to make them feel like intruders. Of course this is not easy for the priest, but it is his job and he must perform it in the best way that he can. He must think of the reactions and the outlook of all his people. In the middle ages, when the townsfolk went into the cathedral for a solemn festival, they would group themselves around the banner of their guild or corporation. There they had their own chapel, dedicated to the patron saint of their guild. In it there would be a stained glass window depicting not only their saint but themselves also, engaged in their various kinds of work. They were really at home, and they knew it.

Parish priests must (it is their duty) see to it that the church pleases the people, and edifies them, by which one means, instructs and educates them. It does not need much imagination to see how appalled some not very highly paid worker must be when he sees row upon row of collecting boxes at the church door. Then there are the irrelevant notices and posters, the fussy hangings and ornaments, the overloaded altars with their artificial flowers, the hideous statues in candy pink and royal blue. No one has the right to ask people with any aesthetic sense to accept such horrors as valid representations of our Lord and his saints.

Our churches should be a faithful picture of our religion, which is true, simple, comforting, and eternal. It is up to the parish priest to see that the picture is a faithful one. He need not be an artist. His task is simply to feed his people spiritually. He cannot treat the church as he may his own house, furnishing it entirely to his own taste. He must remember first that his church is God's house, and as such must be beautiful and dignified. It must bear some reflection of, and be a witness to, God's goodness and greatness. Then again it is the house of God's people, and his twentieth century people at that. No one denies the beauty of the primitive or the Romanesque, but a priest has no right to consider his church as an opportunity for displaying his appreciation of the arts. He is not called upon to startle the world by a fascinating new manifestation of what our modern painters can do when motivated by a Christian impulse. His task is to make prayer easier for his parishioners, not to attract a multitude of art lovers. He should instruct his flock, and art must be his servant, not his master, whatever the critics may think, or say, about him.

His church is for his people and no one else. It is for the whole parish, and not for a chosen few. If he must put anyone first, it must be the humblest and simplest. I do not deny that the churches at Assy and Vence, which have given rise to considerable controversy, may very well suit the people for whom they were designed, but I know very well that they would not do for my parishioners at Colombes! In a parish where there is a very mixed population one must try, however hard it may be, to please them all.

During the German occupation, the Vichy government devised a scheme for employing artists who would otherwise have no work, by getting them to make windows, statues and paintings for the churches. At my church at Petit-Colombes I had always wanted a fresco of the Sacred Heart over the high altar. This, I thought, was my opportunity. An artist was sent to look at the church, and in due course he gave me his suggested design. I admit I am no artist, but in any case I cannot see that an artist's reactions were necessary. Surely, what I thought of it as a parish priest was more important? However, not wishing to be too much influenced by my own judgement, even as a priest, I got together a small committee, not only representative of all the sorts of people in the parish, but composed of the more open-minded and enlightened members. When they saw the design they were quite unanimous. "What do they take us for, Father?", was the general reaction . . . "You asked for the Sacred Heart, and that's what we want – the Sacred Heart, not some demon like this!" I had to agree that that was exactly what it did look like – a demon. Needless to say there is still no fresco over the high altar.

It is so important that the people of the parish should like their church, and that it be something that is within their comprehension. A priest must think of the simplest, the least educated, and think of them, not as children or mental defectives, but as real people. He must think of the parish as a whole. It is not enough to attract the few, because a church is of its nature a place into which people come to be together. It must attract them collectively. It must be the sort of place where they appreciate and realize their brotherhood, where they are glad to pray and sing together, and to be together in our Lord's presence.

This brings us to the priest's place, in the centre of the gathering. He must be there to welcome them. The first bond that links the Christian community together is the priest's own welcoming smile, making them all feel at home, and drawing them together. It is the sincerity and depth and warmth of his prayer that will inspire them as they pray together. He has to be the match that kindles the fire of their love. What could be more natural than that the priest should be at the church door, before the service begins, welcoming his people in fathering them, seeing that they get good places to sit? If anyone should laugh about this, the priest can rest perfectly assured that he is doing something which is too valuable to allow him to bother about comments. He is showing that he cares about his people, and that is the first step towards making their worship a living reality, beneficial to them and something they enjoy.

It is the priest's job not only to see that the church is clean and attractive, but that the liturgy is something alive, a real gathering of people at prayer. What we have said for the church goes for the liturgy too. It is fatal for a priest to follow his own taste exclusively when he is trying to make the liturgy a living thing for all his parishioners. He must remember, once again, that they belong to the twentieth century, and not to the past. They are people who work in factories, who live in an age of scientific discovery, whose crises and sufferings are on an international scale, with world wars to contend with, and political regimes that deny their liberty, and an inclination to think of themselves, and each other, in categories of the class war. All these people must be helped, by the priest, to pray as a body, without any distinction of social class or background. There is no true liturgy, no true worship, without a community praying together.

I was told of one priest who translated a piece from one of Saint Paul's epistles, for a new missal designed to meet the needs of people in a country parish. He showed it to a fellow priest for his opinion of the translation. After reading it, his colleague replied, "As a translation it is very exact and very clear, but it loses the liturgical flavour". Alas for a liturgy that needs liturgical tastes on our part before we can appreciate it! If this were really so, it could be neither popular, nor suited to the general mission field. For a priest, the liturgy simply means making his people pray in union with the whole Church. Its themes and formulas are laid down already, but he has to see that they all centre around Christ. This is the only way to get a praying Church.

If our church services are to be understood by the laity, whose needs they are intended to supply, they must be adapted here and there. A great deal has already been done, with the new popular missals (now better translated), simple altars, mass facing the people, community singing in the vernacular, prayer-leaders, and so on. Let no one think that we are trying to pull down the canons of the Church. We want to make the Church accessible to the people of our time.

Sunday is the Lord's day. It may or may not be a day of

great joy for a parish priest. It may be a day of great disappointment and discouragement. In country districts, for instance, attendance at Mass may be restricted to one or two elderly women, lost in their own private devotions. The priest may have to say several Masses, in a series of such churches, each Sunday. He may have been working himself to the bone during the week, and a little encouragement would do him much good, but none is forthcoming. It takes a long time to see any improvement, and there seems to be less on Sunday than on any other day.

In a big, populous parish, Sunday can be a great event. The priest is with his people, in the very midst of them, sharing their interests and their preoccupations, rousing up their prayer. Each year brings a host of new faces into his congregation, and they can all see him at the church door after Mass, for a few words. He can take the pulse of his parish on a Sunday. He is part of the church, sharing in its usefulness in the lives of these people. It was made for them and so was he. He shares its purpose – the worship of God and his eternal life. Sunday, for him, is indeed the Lord's day.

Nowadays, few priests are likely to be fooled into the belief that people can be attracted to church by anything but the living worship of God. Music may still attract those who might otherwise not come, and the propaganda type of sermon. But what is the point of their carrying away from church some completely profane impression, and pleasures merely for the ear?

The parish priest has to be just as welcoming to those who come to church less frequently, of course. And there are quite a lot of them, who only appear for baptisms, marriages, and burials. There are unfortunately very many, who only meet him on these occasions . . . god-mothers, godfathers, and friends of the family, witnesses, and young relatives. For the non-practising, it is even more important that he should appear as something more than an official personage, going through the motions of some rite which they do not in any case understand, and in which they are frankly not interested. Baptisms, marriages and funerals, like any other church service, are meant to be prayer gatherings. But who is going to see that they pray if it is not the priest himself? When a child is baptized, he has a wonderful opportunity to speak of the Christian life. At marriages everyone will be glad to hear him speak about the place of love in God's plans for mankind. At a funeral, he can give consolation by speaking of our great Christian hope that triumphs over death. On each occasion, there is a chance given him for opening the eyes of the indifferent, and making an appeal to their hearts. It often happens in precisely this way that the most indifferent discover how much nearer to God they are than they had supposed. But it depends so much on whether or not their priest is a welcoming sort of person. Perhaps it is not too extravagant to say that the capacity to welcome people should be one of the priest's great virtues. It is certainly the key to fulfilling his mission among men. No matter who these are – the virtuous ones who never miss Mass, the not-so-virtuous who come when they feel like it or the casual callers at the presbytery door – all must feel that they are welcome. A priest's day is full of encounters, as we shall see in our next chapter. In the street he meets many people he knows, who expect him to remember them and pass the time of day with them. Then of course he has his visiting, which means more meetings with all sorts of people. His welcome must be more than the ability to smile nicely and be a patient listener. He must listen to what they have to say with all his human feelings, because he is called upon to share their lives, make their problems his own, bear their burdens, and be with them always. For he is their shepherd and they are his flock.

The French custom, as I have said, is for the bishop's delegate to show the new parish priest round the church, in public, installing him in the new place which is henceforward his responsibility. During this little ceremony, he takes him to the pulpit, symbolizing that his mission is to *teach* the faithful. "Teaching!" many parishioners might exclaim incredulously . . . "you would never believe it if you heard any of his sermons!" For many, the sermon is the only really dreary thing about their Sunday worship. They often wonder what is the point of sitting there while he rambles on and on. Obviously it is his duty, or he would not do it. And it is their duty, they suppose, to sit quietly until he has finished. If they can manage to have a short sleep in the meantime, so much the better. Unfortunately not a few priests share their opinion.

This is a pity. Obviously, if the sermon is too deep, too abstract, or too high flown, the congregation are justified in their reaction. If his sermons are no more than a course of theology that drifts above their heads week after week, their boredom is not to be wondered at. I remember the story of the preacher who was getting thoroughly warmed up to his subject while the audience remained cold and impassive. He burst out, reproachfully, "My dear brethren, you must realize that I'm not just preaching, I'm telling you the truth!". But so often the truth may have no effect on people because it is wholly unrelated, in its expression, to their lives.

The parish priest's job is to show people how to live the gospel now, in the twentieth century. General rules are not enough, because they can apply to everyone, and therefore affect no one. Dogma remains unchanged, always, everywhere, but the way in which it is taught must obviously differ for varying congregations. Whether his listeners are cultivated or not, they expect their priest to rouse up their faith, kindle their charity, stimulate and enliven their religion. This being the case, he must know what sort of lives they are living. Having once imbibed his dogma and moral course, his preaching can only be prepared during his daily, yearly contacts with his people. His sermons must be steeped in their daily round, and composed of situations which they can recognize as their own.

When they hear him preaching, they must feel immediately that he knows them, and the lives they are living. They must never be allowed to think "This doesn't concern me . . . ." However harsh his criticisms may be, however demanding he may make the gospel sound (after all, its demands are very far reaching) they must be left in no doubt that it is they of whom the gospel speaks.

There is the story of the parish priest who preached so movingly that the whole congregation was in tears – all but one man. Someone, remarking this, asked him whether the sermon had not seemed moving to him. "As a matter of fact, no", he answered, "you see, I don't belong to this parish". A nice point, that could be taken in two ways. It could imply that the people were in the habit of being led by the nose, all doing everything together because their priest had such a hold over them. But it could also mean that the priest had summed up his people so exactly and was so familiar with the local conditions, that an outsider would be lost in so much topicality, and in so precise an analysis of local conditions.

Priests have to remember, too, that it takes time to prepare a good sermon. Improvisations will not really do. One can never forget that the Curé d'Ars always prepared his Sunday sermon throughout a whole week's visits to the Blessed Sacrament. There are other good methods, such as a group preparation, at which several priests decide on the subject together, then later pool their ideas. Finally, each submits his sermon to the criticism of the whole group. The Sunday sermon is something that a priest can be preparing all the time during the course of the preceeding week.

His parishioners, too, can be a help. Not only must they listen with real attention to what he is saying. They can also help him greatly by telling him in which questions they have the greatest interest, which problems trouble their consciences, with which situations they find it most difficult to cope. They need the light of the gospel in their lives, and they can make it easier for their priest to help them if, instead of offering him undeserved congratulations to his face, and unconstructive criticism behind his back, they tell him honestly what they want to know, and in which way his sermons fail to give them what they need, if this be the case. They have every right to receive instruction of a sort that suits their needs. Some can help themselves by their reading, but very many never receive any serious adult education in the faith after they leave school.

If his preaching is impressive by its sincerity, a parish priest can be assured that echoes of his sermons will even find their way into those corners of the parish where people are not so serious in their churchgoing. If the non-practising members of his flock discover that he is a man who is keenly interested in their problems and actually helps his people to bear their burdens, his message will reach even those who are most disinclined to listen. His preaching can reach further than he might suppose. In periods of crisis, people very soon find out which side their priest is on. If he is really facing up to the difficulties encountered by the people of his parish, in matters concerning working conditions, wages, strikes and the rest, he may have to take sides. If, as he should, he comes to the defence of those whom society exploits and neglects, his sermons will find an audience much larger than the one that heard him preaching at Sunday Mass. The experiment of organizing group meetings where the priest can contact people who would normally not hear him in church, has proved successful.

Preaching should take in a wider field, and its appeal should be deepened. It may already be sufficiently aimed at the particular sort of people that compose the parish, but even so it remains a message on the general level, because addressed to all. The word of God, however, must be directed at the individual, as well as the mass. The preacher ought first to bear in mind the whole community, and then consider each individual, helping him to discover God's wishes in his particular case, and to draw conclusions that are personal to him alone. The preacher must enlighten their minds, but he must also stimulate their wills, so that conviction can be translated into practice. He must be a director of consciences, to use the normal and slightly repulsive cliché (consciences being not so much directed as helped and enlightened). The individual thus "directed" still has his own responsibility. He may follow the priest's guidance if he wishes, but he is not bound to do so. The priest is not there to make decisions for his people, but to help them decide for themselves. He has to unravel the tangle that occurs in so many lives, between duty and self-interest, to which are added false ideas and momentary whims.

Priests acting as chaplains to some branch of Catholic Action have precisely this function. Laymen, as we have already pointed out, must accept their responsibilities, and the clergy have no right to meddle in what is properly the task of laymen. What these responsibilities are, the priest must explain. How often will people say, "Father, you're always telling us about religion having to come more into our lives. What do we have to do?" Yet a priest cannot tell each man what his exact duty is. He can only – and he ought to do no more – educate his parishioners so that they may see for themselves what they have to do in any particular circumstance. There is therefore a need to adapt his teaching to the particular social group to which it is addressed.

This brings us to the particular mission which the priest has to fulfil in the social and community life of the parish in which he will often have to deal with questions of conscience posed by individuals, or by the group at large. Problems will differ, for instance, between employers and employees, and these will therefore have to be taken separately, although subjected to the same criterion, which is the gospel.

Some people deplore any partitioning of the parish, however good the reason may be, on the grounds that a parish is a single unit because its members are united through their baptism and through receiving communion at Mass. Others maintain that, if there are to be groups, they must include everybody, however different their personal problems may be. This apparently laudable obsession with unity is, however, a snare. To take the simple example of my car, when it breaks down, I can do one of two things. I can either look at the the engine as a whole, to see what is wrong with it (and that is going to get me nowhere), or I can take the engine to pieces, and find out whereabouts things have gone wrong. It is the same with any modern parish, which, however depressing the comparison may be, is best likened to the human body in the throes of some illness. Overall action is good, but an analysis of each part is far better, and is in fact the only way in which we can get a true, living religion, based on the gospels, circulating throughout the whole body, because that will restore health to each particular member.

As far as the sacraments and liturgy are concerned, obviously the parish can be treated as a unity. The spiritual life of the parish is one and the same for all, but our problem is how to translate this life into the daily round of each individual. Catholic group movements have been one of the biggest factors in the religious revival of our times. The study circles of thirty or fifty years ago, which were open to all, certainly helped. At that time, nothing more could have been attempted. But to-day, with the sharp divisions that exist between so many members of our society, even more specialization has to go into the task of making the gospel known.

Some priests have been shocked to find that a completely new set of tactics was required. It was not enough, they discovered, simply to call an existing group "Young Christian Workers" or "Young Christian Students". Others, on the contrary, were so convinced that here was something entirely new, that they insisted on forming a group at all costs, and then fitting into it those whom they decided would benefit by it. The sensible thing to do was first to get some people interested and active, and then form the group with them as its nucleus. A particularly sore point was the fact that often these groups were organized by some authority outside the immediate parish circle, and meetings would take the parishioners outside their normal confines, and outside the domain of the parish priest. Some priests were absolutely scandalized when their young people attended group meetings outside the parish, instead of coming to Sunday benediction. At first only the really broadminded could accept the fact that they came back stimulated, strengthened, more alive and active, as a result of meeting people from other walks of life, with other ideas, and new approaches. Some found their own parish, by comparison, altogether too stuffy and rigid, and did not fail to say so!

A special effort, and a certain amount of humility, are prerequisites for the priest who attends group meetings. The technique is bound to be different. When he addresses any of his familiar local societies he has a certain section of the parish before him. He organizes the time they spend together in the way he thinks fit. But when he is in contact with the young people in a Catholic Action group, he is bound to find that he is not only asked to speak but, also, and possibly even more, to listen. Often he is called upon to wind up the evening's discussion, having to admit that neither he nor they can as yet put a valid answer to the problems discussed. All this demands humility and self-denial, but it is enormously valuable and worthwhile to the priest, as well as to the people. Priests have thus made contact with people and problems whose existence they had never before suspected . . . *real* worker's problems and the need to do something about them *now*. They can find out as much and more through such a genuine exchange of ideas with young workers, as they could by working in the factories themselves.

Formerly, study circles were by comparison too much attached to the theoretical approach, the handbook and the manual of social studies. What we really need is that different social groups and groups of the same type from different districts, be confronted with each other's problems. This specialized sort of Catholic Action is only just beginning. It is a missionary activity, and it has in some cases already carried whole parishes along with it. We can look forward to some magnificent results when a whole generation of parish clergy has realized its necessity.

We always think of the priest's fundamental teaching activity as being among the children. In practice, in most parishes, it is usually the adults who are in most need of religious instruction. Nevertheless, it belongs to the duty of a priest, as teacher, to instruct the children in the catechism.

Catechism does not mean, we hope, making children recite parrot fashion a string of formulas which mean nothing to them. It means making them aware of what the gospel asks of them, and forming them in good habits of Christian living. In the days when every family was Christian, and children were taught their catechism by their parents, it only required the catechist or priest to check up on the completeness of the teaching received. At the present time, when children coming to catechism cannot even make the sign of the cross, it is a different story. They must be prepared to live what they are taught, and this means teaching them in language they can understand and memorize easily.

In France, first communion seems to be considered as a sort of guarantee that a child has been completely instructed in the faith. One might think that the parish priest must be the happiest man in the world on that occasion, surrounded by so many angelic children looking sweet in their festive clothes. It is, however, more than likely that he is thinking of how many of them, who until now have been regular churchgoers, will henceforth begin to fall away. This is the moment when they solemnly swear to do their best to be good Christians, but in reality they will, over the years, gradually disappear.

It is perhaps far better to make the children see clearly for the first time that they have come into full membership of the Christian community. Instead of presenting first communion as a solemn promise to serve God individually, it can be shown to be something more profound, namely an undertaking to help each other to become good Christians. First communion cannot be an end to the instructions received. There will always be the need for instruction, of a type suited to their age. The first communion dress worn by a girl of twelve, will look ridiculous on her at eighteen. The same thing is true of religious instruction. At the age of twenty, we need something different from that which we were given while still at school. At every age, the parish priest has a responsibility for the religion they are taught. It is not his job to organize their games and camps and theatricals, even though nowadays it may seem that this is a sure way of exerting his influence over them. It is his job to teach them their faith, during their schooldays (as is done in France), and later on, after leaving school, during their professional training or apprenticeship. If the priest neglects this task, no one else will take it on himself. The factories themselves can produce sports clubs and swimming pools, and better ones than the parish can afford, with its limited resources. But no one can replace the priest when it comes to preaching the word of God.

It is the priest's essential function to give the sacraments. Of baptism, the first, we have already spoken. The second and the greatest is the Eucharist, which is given to the faithful every time the sacrifice of Calvary is repeated. After Mass the Eucharist is reserved in the tabernacle. The priest has not only to care for the fabric of his church but also for the divine presence dwelling therein. He is especially responsible for the tabernacle. The possibility of profanation exists and the parish priest has to take every precaution against that happening: also against theft. Above all, however, his is the task of keeping alive devotion to our Sacramental Lord among the faithful, and encouraging them to visit the Blessed Sacrament frequently.

This is important even in parishes where there are few practising Catholics and where very few are likely to spare the time for a visit. Even if this is so, a priest knows that our Lord is there, in his church, and even if no one else comes, the priest cannot do without the presence of his Master. My first parish priest was later appointed vicar-general, and he told me that one day, when visiting a parish unexpectedly, he found the sanctuary lamp unlit and the tabernacle empty. He asked the priest about it and received the reply: "What's the use? No one ever comes in here during the day." The vicar-general being a wise and holy man replied: "Yes . . . but even so, what about yourself? Even if it is an extra expense, keeping the lamp alight, surely you can count that as a little luxury that you can't do without!"

Then there is the confessional. Another heavy job. We give absolution but we can do more. If the penitent can be encouraged to take his confession seriously, and do something more than repeat his list of habitual sins, the priest can really help. If he can follow some trend in the penitent's life, through his confessions, like a doctor who follows the ups and downs of a patient's health, he can do a great amount of good. The important thing, as the Abbé Godin used to say, is to be like those country priests who know everybody *and* everything about everybody.

One of the greatest consolations a priest can give is his ministration to the sick. And by this I mean something more than waiting until the last minute before turning up with the Last Sacrament. He should visit all the sick who cannot get to church. How else can he "preach" to them? And besides, there is a very special gospel message for them, and a very special way in which our Lord invites them to live the gospel.

The sick, in any parish, are a community on their own. At least they can be, if the priest cares to bring them together. If he visits them all and knows them all, they get to know each other through him. They can pray for each other, take an interest in each other, and be of great help to one another without actually meeting at all. If he cares to, he can build up in this way a wonderful back-bone of solid prayer in the parish, to help him in his work, and the people of the parish and indeed all Christians everywhere, since their suffering and sacrifice is all a part of the Redemption of this world. It would be very sad to think of the sick in our parishes as so many burdens, so many inactive and therefore useless people. On the super-natural level, which is the level that counts most, they are the first, because they are united to our Lord on his cross.

Such, briefly, are a parish priest's main tasks. There is, however, one constant temptation lying in wait for him. This is the ease with which he can be taken in by appearan-ces. He is called upon to witness for God, and for the invisible order, in a society which is thoroughly pagan and materially minded. He is a man like other men, and like them he can quite easily be swept along with the rest. The grace received in Holy Orders does not render him immune from the dangers that come with perpetual contact with values alien to his state.

He can so easily be led away from the essential things in his ministry. He will have much administrative matter to deal with, building perhaps, good works of all sorts, clubs and societies and meetings – all useful, but none of it either first or foremost. All the while he has to try to live an inner life, to think in terms of real values, trying to pray, to concentrate on keeping his mind on God, keeping his vision fresh and alive. The only thing that is absolutely essential for him is to give Christ to men, and to preach his word to them. And for this there is no substitute.

As a man gets older, he tends to become more and more the slave of the things he himself produces. He can become a little creator in his own right, and turn away from his master without realizing it, because he has got into the habit of thinking of his life as his own achievement, instead of seeing it as something he has done in conjunction with God. Perhaps this explains why we find men going through a crisis in their religious lives between thirty and forty, because they have become self-sufficient and make less room in their lives for God. Priests, too, particularly parish priests, can make the same mistake. They can tend to think that everything depends on them alone. That is why the parish can do a useful service by asking the priest to ensure, not that they get parish halls and football grounds, but true Christian charity radiating throughout the community.

The faithful have no right to expect their parish priest to give them things of a material nature. What they can and must ask of him is to wake them up to the gospel and its demands in their lives, and keep them faithful to those demands. A priest need ask for nothing more but to have his mission understood in this light, and to have the help of the parish in fufilling his mission. His people can remind him of his most essential task. They can remind him of the reason why he became a priest in the first place, and why the bishop appointed him to a parish.

Chapter Six

A PRIEST'S DAY

WHEN, as a child, I used to tell my mother how much I wanted one day to be a priest, she would always laugh and say, "Well I'm not surprised! It's the sort of lazy life you'd like!" This attitude was typical of our part of the world, where the priest's day was imagined to be a sort of vacuum between morning Mass and whatever might be going on in the evening. During the day there would be nothing to do but perform an occasional marriage or funeral.

When I eventually became a priest, a cousin of mine one day complained that I had failed to answer his letter. When I said I had been too busy, he obviously could not believe me. "Too busy?" he asked. "But you've nothing to do all day!" I was reminded of the French priest who was caught opening the presbytery shutters at the end of a hot summer day. A boy was just turning in at the gate and he said, quite seriously, "It must be nice to sleep all day. After all, Father, you've only got the children's catechism to teach, haven't you? If we didn't come to see you, why you'd have nothing to do at all!"

That is what they think of the priestly life. "That

wonderful life", as one author put it, "monotonous and absolutely pointless." So, in order to dispel a popular misconception, I feel I must write a chapter describing a typical day in a priest's life. It is neither useless nor monotonous. It is, in fact, full of variety. This is a random selection of things that may happen during the day.

Let us imagine that the priest rises at half past six. I am not suggesting that this is a general rule, or even an ideal time for a priest to get out of bed. In the seminary we acquired the habit of rising at half past five, but in those days our programme was very different. To-day it is the priest's evenings that are busiest, with meetings to attend, clubs and other activities, visiting and so on. Usually priests get to bed late. Generally speaking, the life of the parish does not begin until the evening, since it is only when they return from work that people are free to dispose of their time in the way they prefer, and to get down to the things they really want to do, whether they feel inclined to amusement, serious study, some apostolic work, or even prayer. This is the time when a priest can be very busy indeed, because he can be sure of meeting everybody. Therefore, if he does not get to sleep before midnight, it is hardly likely that he will feel like rising at half past five.

There are days when he wishes there were no need to get

up until much later! Sometimes, if he is to get in as much sleep as the average monk or nun (to make a comparison with people who do not get a great deal of sleep), he would need to stay in bed until at least eight o'clock, but he has his Mass to say, and this is always scheduled for a fixed time, to suit the convenience of the parishioners. Not that he can expect many people to come to Mass every day, because the circumstances of their lives make this impossible – mothers with homes to look after, children off to school, workers starting early. . . . No other society would think of holding its meetings between half past six and eight in the morning, but the Church moves slowly, and we can only hope that evening Masses will become more and more frequent.

A priest usually likes to spend half an hour, not only preparing for his Mass, but putting his whole day in God's hands. The Mass is the most important thing in his life, and it is for this that he is first and foremost responsible in the life of the parish. Every morning he offers his work and all his troubles to the Lord, offering them with the host so that they may be our Lord's work, and our Lord's responsibility.

The parish should be a unit, and the priest's mission is to see that it remains so. He must bring unity into the family, and among families, and throughout the district which he looks after. Human nature, however, being what it is, this ideal unity is always being disrupted by enmity, selfishness, jealousy and pride, from one day's end to another. And so the priest thanks the Lord that he has the Mass, for this is the Lord's own way of making us one, gathering us into the unity of the divine life. Every morning, no matter how disappointing the preceding day, no matter how much he is tempted to say, like Saint Vincent de Paul, "I shall never succeed", the priest knows that our Lord is there in the very heart of his parish, binding the people together. In the Mass, every morning, it is our Lord who sends his grace to overcome human selfishness and the forces of evil. And in the end, every priest knows, our Lord will triumph.

The priest goes up to the altar with the whole parish in his heart. Even if he is alone in church, he is with them all.

After Mass he makes his thanksgiving. Perhaps there are confessions to be heard. While he is praying near the altar, the people know that he is ready to see anyone who wishes to see him. That, after all, is what he is there for. An old lady will come and ask him to call and see her husband this afternoon, because he is not at all well. A young man on his way to work drops in to ask him if he may call this evening, or to-morrow. He sees someone in the church with whom he particularly wants to have a talk, and stops him on the way out. Sometimes it may mean a longer interview in his office. This is happening at what is technically breakfast time. It would be nice to spend a little time with the paper, and his correspondence. As it is he can probably only glance at the headlines and read his letters through quickly, before he is called away. This time it may be the housekeeper who wants him to look at the accounts, or to tell him that the stove is not working probably, or that there is a leak somewhere. He promises to do something about it. Then there is someone at the door.

It is a problem with which he is very familiar, and so he must be careful to be more than usually attentive. An unfortunate young wife whose husband is always drunk . . . last night he was worse than usual, and no one had any sleep before four in the morning, and the children were all terrified. They are still too frightened to eat – not that she has very much to give them, because she gets hardly any money. Nothing new in this situation, but now things are so bad that it is obvious that, for the children's sake at least, she will have to leave her husband. This means a host of new questions to discuss. Where shall she go, what sort of work can she do, who will look after the children while she is at work? Advice needs to be carefully thought out, and this takes time. Quite a large portion of the morning has been taken up by this one interview alone. When she has gone, our parish priest has hardly opened his breviary before someone else wants to see him.

The next visitor is obviously a beggar. You can tell by the look of him, before he starts to tell you that he hasn't eaten for two days, or that he's lost his job, or that he hasn't enough money to get to Paris, or that he's just come out of hospital, or prison. Some are genuine and some are frauds, and there is no end to the ingenuity of their hard-luck stories. A postal order is on the way; could Father lend a small sum until it comes? A man, having nearly murdered his unfaithful wife, wants to escape to Switzerland; could Father give him the money for the fare . . .? It may be a down-and-out Negro who says he hasn't the money to get his bag out of the customs, or a taximan who has driven into a shop window, and wants to pay immediately because he is not insured. At first one can never be absolutely sure who is genuine and who false. Sometimes, because he would rather risk being deceived than leave someone in real need, and also because he cannot spare the time to enquire too deeply into the matter, he gives.

Next comes a surprise visitor, a woman who never comes to church and who asks the priest, to his great surprise, to take her little boy in his catechism class. "But surely" he asks, "you realize that he will be taught to do all sorts of things you don't bother to do yourself – firstly, to go to Sunday Mass." He has to show her, and many another mother with as little logic, that by sending a child to catechism class, the parents are themselves taking on an obligation. It is a delicate point to discuss, and again, it takes time.

After this, he makes another attempt to say his office. Then the telephone rings. They want to know at the town hall if he will come to a meeting connected with the Tuberculosis Fund. Then a request from the Red Cross, asking if he will take a collection next Sunday for coal for the old folk. Then another knock at the door. This time it is someone looking for lodgings. This is the moment when he starts to despair. Even for an urgent case he can promise no definite help. How many times already, for equally urgent cases, has he sought all over the place, and written here and telephoned there. And yet, curiously enough, when it seemed hopeless, he usually found something in the end.

The really awful request, however, has yet to come. "Please Father, they told my husband that if you would give him a reference, he would be able to get a job at the factory." It is heartbreaking for a priest to be thus innocently suspected of working hand in glove with the employers. However much he may insist that he knows neither the directors nor the personnel manager, it is a question of daily bread for a whole family. They don't believe him, and he can't refuse. So he writes the reference, feeling miserable.

The next few visitors are women who drop in on the way back from a morning's shopping. They have nothing important to say, but he has to be polite. Fortunately there is no one else waiting to see him, because when there is, and his time is engaged by these good ladies who have so little reason for wasting it, it is very difficult not to be rude to them.

Midday arrives and he has perhaps been unable to say his office, or write his letters, or keep his promise to the housekeeper, or make any of the telephone calls he had in mind . . . no time for study, no time for prayer, no time to go and see two or three people who said they wanted to see him. And yet he knows time must be set aside for all these things. To-morrow perhaps? And at his next retreat, as at all the others, he will resolve very firmly to do something about his programme, to make it more spiritual, to give more time to pursuits of the mind.

After lunch he can get down to one essential at least – the breviary – but he has to be quick about it because someone is sure to call in on the way back to work. In the afternoon he goes visiting. Perhaps he goes to see a contractor or two before calling on the sick. There is poor X. who has been paralysed for twenty years, to whom even a short visit means so much. There is a young woman with tuberculosis at an age when all her friends are getting married and having families. She needs consolation, and the least word that can give her hope. He is buttonholed by a young woman as he passes the door of her flat. "We've been wanting to speak to you for a long time, Father! Can't you come round one evening?" He makes a note in his engagement book. In another house he meets someone else who has been wanting to talk to him for a long time, this time about her son's future. "What sort of job would he be best at Father? Where are some good openings, Father, I'm sure you know . . . " And so it goes on.

It is unlikely that he has completed his agenda by the end of the afternoon, which means by five o'clock on three days a week, on account of the catechism class. It is round about this time that he likes to make a visit to the Blessed Sacrament, to talk over what has happened thus far in his day with the Lord – to ask for light and strength, and above all energy to carry on to the busiest part of his day. This is the time when young couples come to see him about getting married. They are not always completely at their ease with the priest, particularly those who have not even been baptized or made their first communion. There is a lot to talk about because marriage is such an important step. It would be wrong, one feels, to look at it as just another session of form-filling. This is not just a civil affair, rather it is a great opportunity for showing young people all that is involved in Christian love and family life, because, under the influence of their affection for each other, they are able to see further than the ordinary perspective of their all too familiar daily round. Marriage, they discover perhaps for the first time, is more to the Church than the giving of a blessing. It is the cementing of a lifetime bond, and as such needs thorough deliberation and real understanding of what the contract implies.

At six o'clock the offices and factories are closing and he must expect all kinds of callers. There may be one or two tragic cases, like the man who arrives in a terrible state to say his wife has deserted him and left him with their two children. The parish priest has to help sort out the problem of where to put the children in the meantime, how to get in touch, if possible, with the wife. They must, at least, try to bring her back, and this alone may take – and often does – weeks of patient enquiry and persuasion. Then, when there is a chance of putting the marriage right again, the problem will be more difficult than any which arose in the early days of marriage, which, God knows, are difficult enough.

Between six and eight, the waiting room is fullest. With dinner at eight, the day is far from ended. In fact, the most important part of the day is just beginning. Evening is the time for meetings, in various places of the parish, for a variety of reasons, and any of them capable of going on until about eleven. Followed of course by further conversations and confidences, some of the most useful and significant of the whole day, and therefore not to be minimized. With a sigh, he remembers that his correspondence is still untouched. There are still hosts of important questions unanswered, urgent business still left undone . . . to say nothing of preparing a sermon, or reading an important article, or reviewing a book, doing the accounts or getting material ready for the parish magazine. To-morrow perhaps? Even that is unlikely, when there is a meeting of the clergy in the morning and a conference (still unprepared) to be delivered to the women's guild in the afternoon. The next day then . . . ? Let us see, Wednesday. Probably the whole day will be spent in finding a suitable place for the children's summer camp. Thursday – the children again, and their parents. Friday? Perhaps, unless it turns out to be a day like to-day when there was scarcely a free minute. Saturday, there will be marriages in the morning, and the afternoon will bring him all the callers who could not manage to come during the week, and then the confessional from five onwards. And so far no mention of burials, baptisms, odd jobs in the presbytery, material preoccupations of different

kinds, and always the unexpected. . . . Father is not
agitating for an eight-hour day. An eight-hour night
would be more to his advantage! Sunday is far from
being a day of rest, but if he has any sense he will see
to it that he gets away for one day each week – to get as
far away as possible from that door bell and all that it
may entail during the course of a day.

The country clergy are, of course differently situated.
The rhythm of life in the country is different, for the
priest as well as for everyone else. But quite often a
priest in a rural area is responsible for several parishes,
which means that he has to cover a lot of ground to
assure Sunday Mass for everyone, and catechism, and
meetings and visits and so on. He is kept out late on winter
nights, and he is usually less able to get other people to
do his odd jobs for him. He is his own sacristan, his own
church cleaner, his own housekeeper and handyman,
simply because his small budget does not allow him to do
otherwise. The pretty picture of the parish priest, saying
his breviary in a quiet corner of his garden, is very much
a thing of the past!

I do not suggest for a minute that all priests are busy
and enthusiastic. That depends on their temperament and
their energy and their generosity. Some begin their
priestly life at such a feverish pace that it is virtually

impossible to keep it up. Others lose interest little by little and become wrapped up in themselves. Some eventually dedicate themselves exclusively to some sideline, and yet others to an endless perusal of the daily papers. But a priest who keeps his eyes open and can see what needs to be done, is not likely to have much time for himself.

Chapter Seven

THE PARISH PRIEST

AND THE WORLD OF TO-DAY

THE fundamental paradox in any priest's life is that he is not of the world, but at the same time his work must make its mark on the world. Our Lord asked his Father, not to take the apostles out of the world, but to keep them from evil. They were to remain in the world without becoming worldly themselves.

Often a priest has been, as it were, separated from the world at quite an early age, as early as twelve years old, at the junior seminary. This means that he has spent his adolescence and youth in a world apart, with its own special pursuits, inculcating the taste for a special way of life. He would notice the difference during holiday time, and as the abbé Godin remarked, the difference is often one that causes sadness – between his way of life, his way of thinking, and the outlook of his brothers, sisters and friends at home.

The education which priests receive, in a seminary, is a bourgeois education. The culture he imbibes there makes him grow up slowly, so that he matures later than his friends. Children who are brought up in poverty and unhappiness grow up very quickly, as we know from their sad, grown-up, troubled expression. When one has never had any reason for smiling, a scowl soon becomes habitual. At eighteen, these youths have grown up completely. Their daily contacts in the factory or wherever they work, in constant contact with an adult way of life, soon result in their sharing in the obsessions and the worries of their elders.

Students, on the other hand, (including our bourgeois young students for holy orders), rarely mature before the age of twenty-five or thirty. Young people are like trees. They stop growing at different levels. Maturity for a student comes later than it does for a manual worker, and is something different.

Over and above this, a priest develops in an atmosphere devoted to pursuits of the mind. He is brought up on abstractions. He is only familiar with theory, whether it be scientific, philosophical, theological, or mystical. And whereas, until his ordination, he had been trained to look within, to develop his interior life, as soon as he is ordained he has to make a quick change. As a curate, he is suddenly plunged headlong into a completely material world. He is brought down to earth with a bump. Until now he has only observed the world in the pages of books. His principal efforts have been expended on striving after his own spiritual, interior perfection. Now he is surrounded by real life and has to face up to the task of helping others

116

to find their salvation. And it is not just a question of having something to do in this everyday world; his job is to leave his mark on it, to mould it, to help it to develop in the right way, to help raise it up to a higher level. This being the case he has to fit into it, understand it and make it thoroughly his own. His job is to preach the gospel to the twentieth century, and not to some hypothetical generation of yesterday. He has to fight against the abuses of the *present* day, and to shed the light of Christ's message on current problems. What is the good of having all the heresies of the fifth and sixth centuries at his finger ends if he is ignorant of our modern heresies? And what is the good of knowing what was wrong in the Church's approach at the Renaissance if he cannot tell the wheat from the chaff in the ideas which captivate the world to-day?

We have to instill Christianity into men and women of the mid-twentieth century. We cannot speak to them to-day in terms of what was going on even as little as ten years ago, now that the world changes so often and so quickly. Almost every year has its own special needs, and priests must keep up with them.

A priest's education is by no means the only thing that sets him in a world apart. If he is not careful he will find that the parish itself tends to become his whole world, and to cut him off from reality. The abbé Godin has already shown us in his book, *France Pagan?* what a small minority the parish can represent, and how completely ineffectual it can be in reaching the world around it. It is perfectly easy for a priest to be so busy in this little parish world, that he never finds the time or the reason for getting out of it. He will have many people coming to see him, plenty of sick calls, over and above his duties in church, to fill all his days. He will know his flock and they will know him. But here the risk is that he will take this small group of people as being typical of the great world into which he never ventures. His ideas of the different classes and categories of people will all be formed through the few he meets during his parish work. This happens to many priests, and of course they never know it is happening. It is like living in a very stuffy room. Only the people coming into it are assailed by the smell. And the little stuffy room eventually becomes identified with the whole universe.

In France our biggest problem is the working population. The workers are always going to be the biggest proportion of parishioners, so it is imperative that the priest should really understand them. But most French vocations to the priesthood come from other strata of society – many from rural areas (in France it is still no dishonour to call oneself a peasant), from the middle classes, and sometimes from the aristocracy. Very few vocations come from the workers because it was the workers who were lost to the Church in France during the nineteenth century. It is, perhaps, not completely true to say that the proletariat was *lost* to the Church for, in fact, it only came into being outside the Church.

The peasants are the only class which has always belonged to the Church, because they were there even before the Church was founded. The aristocracy was baptized, we might say, during its period of power in the Middle Ages. The artisan class came into the Church when the great corporations were formed, and the bourgeoisie, such as we know it to-day, came in in the nineteenth century, and has not yet been completely converted. There were no industrial "workers", in the modern sense, before the middle of the nineteenth century, and they still have not been baptized.

It is this class with which our priests are least familiar, because it has remained separate from the rest of society. It keeps to its own quarters, is ground down by the sheer fatigue of work, and is an easy prey to any propaganda that works on class distinctions. Its culture is very different from that of the bourgeoisie. It thinks along materialistic lines, and as a collectivity. A priest may imagine that he understands the workers simply because he happens to know one or two of them among his parishioners. These few are, more often than not, no longer of their class, and no longer really belong to it.

The rector of a big suburban parish once told me that his parish could not be considered "working class", "because there are twenty five members in our Saint Vincent de Paul conference, and only one of them works in a factory!" In point of fact, the marriage register alone proved the contrary, with eighty percent of the marriages between factory workers. So it was clear that the parish priest did not know the number of working class people, did not even realize their existence in fact. Is it likely, then, that he would be familiar with their outlook? His whole ministry was inevitably thrown out of balance by this false assessment of the people with whom he was dealing. The remedy was simple enough. He had only to get to know them.

Tragically, the priest is often quite oblivious of his ignorance about the members of his parish. He and the workers speak, all too often, a different language. They do not feel at home in a church; they do not understand the ceremonies, the vestments and, least of all, the sermons. There is a vast barrier of prejudice.

Monsignor Ancel has written: "In the eyes of the workers, the Church is indissolubly linked with capitalism, and consequently with exploitation. Capital is the enemy, and the Church is included under capital. When France was occupied during the war, we all felt an instinctive revulsion every time we saw a German uniform on the streets, and although we might know perfectly well that the wearer of it was a thoroughly good man, none the less the horror occasioned by the mere uniform remained. The workers feel the same way about the priest's black cassock when they meet him on the street. They may know the priest, and like and admire him, but his uniform makes him the enemy of the working class, and that, in their eyes, is enough."

A very different situation prevails in the country, amongst a peasant population. In the first place, the country priest is usually of local origin. He may be the baker's son or the blacksmith's son, but in any case he belongs to the peasant's world. He is familiar with the people, he knows the way they think and feel. He grew up in this little world, which is a self-contained unit, and so it is much easier for him to communicate with them at all times, simply because he, as it were, speaks their language.

In a city parish, however, a priest can live without ever realizing that socially, morally, and intellectually, he is infinitely remote from his people, or at least the greater part of them. The reason is that there may be, in any parish largely composed of factory workers, a larger number of middle-class people coming to his church. And he may easily take them to be the majority. It is this situation that gave rise to the priest-worker movement, and that still gives priests a jaundiced idea of what the parish ministry must be like. Fortunately, when one has spent some years working in a parish, one loses any such doubts about the efficacy of parochial work.

In France there is a colossal gap between the Church and the workers (whether we think of them as having lost the faith, or as never having been baptized into it). Awareness of its existence is something deeply upsetting for any conscientious priest. His task is enormous, well beyond the scope of his powers. He is presented with a vast mission, and he may well wonder where it is best to begin. Young priests get impatient, because they want at all costs to see some achievement. They realize in theory that it will take several generations before any noticeable change can be expected, but in the meantime they want, even if only subconsciously, to see the change already effected. Parish work is always a long-term project. The results of a priest's work are like a scaffolding that goes up very slowly. It is only after years, sometimes twenty or thirty years, that he may see tangible results, some achievement, some progress. Obviously one would prefer to plunge right into the heart of this working society lost to the Church, just as the worker priests have done, in order to take the leaven right into the middle where it is needed.

Another temptation for the priest is to be so closely tied to his theories and ideals that he is never able to apply his mind to concrete fact and circumstance. But his reactions ought to be more than purely intellectual. A worker reacts with his whole being, and his whole life. Whenever he is involved in an argument, a working man seizes on the facts and the things that touch him on all the sore points of his own life and experience. He considers a discussion of ideas a mere waste of time, because he has heard so much propaganda built up on irresistible logic, proof and demonstration. He has heard orators defending contradictory notions so well that neither side could be disproved . . . or so it seemed to him. A sermon or a newspaper article couched in abstract terms has no conviction for him because he expects to be taken in by those whose interest it is to deceive him for some party line or other. But let him only hear someone speaking from experience and his reactions are immediate, because he can share an experience and he knows what it is to want and to suffer.

The priest, for his part, can easily forget these facts of experience which are the really important things in the workers' lives. He will even minimize the present difficulties and shortcomings in society for the sake of a future which he is doing his bit to improve. For the workers, however, it is the present trials which are precisely the yardstick for finding out if the various doctrines propounded for his benefit mean anything at all. If the propagandists can improve his present conditions, all well and good. It is the present that counts, not a hypothetical future. If they can only talk to him about his future, he knows where he can go.

Although French priests are often accused of being too bourgeois (and we admit that the temptation is great, and the accusation often well founded) most middle class people will tell you that the priest does not understand them any more than he does the factory workers. The middle class people whom he knows, that is those who come to church, are probably a rather colourless group. He only knows them insofar as they reveal themselves to him, asking his advice, and coming to him for confession. But apart from this, the parish priest usually knows just as little about the private life of his middle-class parishioners as he does about that of the factory workers, for the simple reason, that he no longer belongs either to the working or to the middle class. He is less removed from the latter because he happens to have had much the same sort of education as they, and has adopted the same social conventions. When they leave school, however, the children of middle-class families go into a world of business which is as remote from the clergy's life as any factory.

There is, furthermore, a diametrical opposition of interests. A priest must have an eye for the interior life, and the things that are not seen. The bourgeois world is a money-making world, aimed at profit and the enjoyment of wealth. If a priest feels more at home in people's drawing rooms over a cup of tea, this is largely because a higher standard of good manners allows all concerned to overlook social differences. On the staircase of some large workers' tenement, however, social differences are uncomfortably obvious. In the middle-class and working-class homes, people often feel that the priest is not one of them. Whether they make a point of shrugging their shoulders with an indifference that they know very well he will notice, or of listening to what he says out of politeness, there is not much difference in the long run. Whether impatient or polite, they do not give much thought to what he says.

Even if there are priests who prefer to sit in the drawing-rooms of the rich because they feel more at home there, this does not imply that their hosts are any more likely to come to church because they feel at home in God's house. It does not imply that they have any more taste for what he has to say than the factory workers have. It certainly does not mean that what he says is any more comprehensible to them than to the less educated!

The truth is that our upper class population is just as irritated by class distinctions that single them out, as are the so-called working classes. They do not want to be thought of as existing in a category apart. They would like to see an end to these tacitly accepted distinctions in the parish. Everyone, regardless of his social position, would prefer to be taught what the gospel teaches, and to be treated in the way that our Lord treated the men and women of his time. A priest is bound to be involved in politics, at least in other people's minds. Whenever a political party that persecutes the Church gets into power, bishops and priests are accused of meddling in politics. They may be imprisoned, tortured, deported as we know well from the history of recent dictatorships. Although we in France have a different conception of liberty, none the less the French people are always on the look out for the least sign of clerical interference in politics. This is quite understandable since in the realm of politics everyone has the right to make his own choice, and none of the conflicting parties can claim to have a monopoly on truth or justice. The Church must respect these facts, but every Christian has to remember that his own conscience in political matters must be guided by principles founded on the gospel.

In the past, admittedly, French priests have taken sides for various forms of government, sometimes contemporary and sometimes out of date. A priest can wield, even now, a great influence in his parish. His influence may weigh heavily on people's consciences. That is why he must be very careful not to identify in his own mind Christian principles and personal preferences. We can say honestly, however, that the clergy has learned a lesson since the French Revolution. There are still royalist outposts in Brittany and the Vendée but not very many. Men are formed, mentally and spiritually, by locally accepted ideas and ideals. The social and political structure of any society must inevitably influence the material and moral welfare of its citizens, but it is very wrong to think that as long as one particular order remains in force, there is nothing further to be done to make the world more Christian. That is why the theorists who hold that, given certain conditions, the working classes will automatically come back to Christ, are as mistaken as some old priest who may stake the conversion of France on the restoration of the monarchy.

A real pastor never minimizes the efficacy of politics, but he will accept two important principles. The first is that in politics, as in any other sphere, there is a Christian and an unchristian way of doing things. A priest's task then is to awaken his people, remind them of their duties,

127

see that they do hold fast to Christian principles, and enlighten those who don't know. As far as immediate action is concerned he will leave the initiative to the people, because this is their business. He ought to be scrupulous about this, and very discreet, his guiding thought being to let them act independently.

His second principle is to put Christ at the beginning, and as the foundation of all that he does, and to make Christ known. This is not only his mission, but it is the most urgent and vital thing for him to do, and it comes before everything else.

Every social group depends upon its members. These alone determine whether or not it can serve any useful purpose, and it will develop usefully only when its impetus comes from some spiritual source. The gospel alone is sufficient leaven to raise up the mass of mankind. If a parish priest preaches Christ, he is laying the foundation stone on which all social and political theory is best built, and he will not be guilty of "clericalism".

There is nothing to stop a priest playing a role in local goverment, or editing a newspaper, if his bishop allows him to do that. A priest is a citizen like any other, with equal rights, but if he engages in this sort of activity, he does so as a citizen, and not as a priest. As a priest, he is the Church's official representative. He is responsible for a small part of the whole Church. As a private citizen, any political activity he undertakes may jeopardize his work as a priest. His spiritual authority gives him a certain power over the minds of others, and therefore he must be most careful that he is not carrying this influence into a field of action where men and women are free in their choice. He ought, at election time, to keep his political opinions to himself when preaching, and give no one cause for mispresenting him. His ministry ought to make him extremely sensitive on this point.

In the years preceding the war, it was normal for French priests to avoid becoming involved in politics by taking up instead, and getting others to take up, an interest in social work. This had the fortunate result of bringing a great many young people into the sphere of social welfare, when they would otherwise have had no effect on society at all, and would have remained at home or tied to their own jobs. In this way many Christians realized, for the first time, their obligations to their fellow men.

Soon, however, this distinction between politics and social work was discovered to be an illusion. Inevitably, to take a stand on social questions means that there will be repercussions in one's political outlook. The problem, as far as priests were concerned, was not an easy one to solve, because moral well-being depends very much on social conditions. The people with whom a priest has to deal, and for whom he is responsible, are either workers or employers, and he has the duty of teaching them about their particular responsibilities and their rights, and the way in which these can be defended.

It is a great temptation for a priest to impose certain rules of conduct. As far as defending the faith goes, everyone must be ready to lay down his life for Christ, and it is the priest's duty to see that people are prepared to make such a sacrifice. They are not, however, to lay down their lives for the particular line he adopts on social questions, and he has no right to ask such a sacrifice from them.

It is not an easy task to expound the Church's teaching as we find it in the encyclicals, underlining the principles involved and seeing to it that each member of the Church is ready to do his duty, but it is not sufficient to present the doctrine as it stands and to quote texts verbatim. A priest must interpret the Church's teaching, because he knows, or should know, precisely what are the factors peculiar to his parish. He should know what his parishioners' reactions will be when confronted with a given situation, what their problems are, and their likes, dislikes and prejudices. His task is to discover the things which are most important and necessary for the needs of these people. To aid him the Church has produced a vast amount of documentary guidance.

A priest's role, moreover, is not so much that of an arbitrator who intervenes in a time of crisis, although this may well fall to his lot. It is far more important for him to instruct his flock consistently, all the time, about their Christian duty, so that they take the Church's teaching to heart and put it into practice. If he does this he can leave it to the people to choose wisely and to act prudently in any crisis. The danger obviously exists that the clericalism of yesterday might merely be superseded by a new clericalism on the part of those young and zealous priests, who tend to be too rigid in the ideas they would impose on their young followers. It is not enough for the laity to be ardent and faithful disciples. They must be trained to achieve maturity of mind and personality, so that they will be capable of standing on their own feet, of facing the truth squarely, and judging and acting in the light of Christian principles, without any prompting from the priest.

Then there is the question of money. I remember an evening in the Bois de Boulogne, where we were sitting after a tiring day. There were some children playing ball beside us, and of course the ball got lost, as it always does. The children started to cry, their parents hunted among the bushes, so we joined in the search. It was one of the curates who found the ball. Everyone was very grateful, and we forgot all about it. A little later, the father of the child who lost the ball came to see the curate, this time with a little thank-offering in an envelope. It was almost impossible to make him understand that we did not want to accept it and that we were sufficiently rewarded by making the child happy. The father was so taken aback by our refusal that I thought I had better explain then and there the way that priests feel about money.

Sure enough, you will find in some French books of the "How to Make Friends and Be Popular" type, a chapter on how to thank people in the right way, how to pay a doctor or a taxi driver, how to give flowers to a lady, and, believe it or not, the right way of giving money to a priest, which includes the remark: "For the poor people in your parish, Father!" Isn't it revolting? After all, if the priest has done anything to earn the money, one can give it to him in the same way that one gives a doctor his fee. If you think he is really poor, then you can give him an alms, making no bones about it. There is no need for circumlocutions, or delicate euphemisms, which only imply, "I know perfectly well that you live on charity, but I can't bring myself to say so". There is no need to think of a priest as someone to whom money is always acceptable, whatever the pretext.

How often it happens in a priest's daily round, when giving some advice perhaps, or after a little talk with someone, that the wallet is taken out, or the handbag is rummaged. It makes the priest wonder what they take him for.

If, as I said, we have done anything to warrant the payment, pay us by all means, but please try not to think of us as being always on the look out for an offering. Of course priests need money, just like everyone else, and many of them cannot make ends meet. A parish priest in Paris may receive as much as eighteen thousand francs a month, a country priest much less than ten thousand. Yet personal finances are a priest's smallest worry. It is the parish finances themselves that are a nightmare, but even then he knows he can rely – as he must – on Providence. On the debit side he can always put "Providence", because he knows that he can, and must, always fall back on the help of this bountiful benefactor who is always incognito, and absolutely dependable.

Over the years, various systems have been devised for stabilizing a priest's income; stole fees, collecting boxes of all sorts, and various tariffs for weddings and funerals. I even heard of a parish where the customary offering for a funeral is a new pall, destined to be made into clothes for the clergy! But nowadays, fortunately, priests do tend to depend more on Providence, and the tariff scheme is disappearing in many places. I have yet to find a priest who suffered financially as a result.

We must never forget that Christ our Lord warned us that we cannot serve two masters. It must be either Christ, or money; it cannot be both. In the world of to-day everything is thought of in terms of hard cash, everything is thoroughly exploited for selfish ends. If the priest can show that he is not interested in money first and foremost, he will create quite an impression. He immediately becomes a mystery man, and people wonder what his motive can be. It must mean that he works because of some conviction that has nothing to do with money. Every working man in France is brought up on the assumption that religion is an invention intended to line priests' pockets, and one can imagine how completely he is taken by surprise when, on enquiring "How much do I owe you for the funeral?", he is told that one doesn't pay for prayers, and that, moreover, there is no need to pay for them even indirectly, disguised as alms or anything else. However indifferent the questioner may be about his religion, he can at least see that his priest is working for Christ, and for no one else.

The most touching story I know, in this context, comes from a curate in Paris, who had to marry two young people who were so poor that, for several months, the fiancé had been sleeping in a railway station. The young woman expected to stay in her parents' home after the marriage, without her husband, because there was no

134

room for him and nowhere for them to go. The young man was not baptized, and came to see the curate several times for instruction. He wanted to be really well prepared for his marriage. Often, when he arrived at the presbytery in the evening, he had had no supper, and was not likely to get any. They knew no one and the witnesses had to be supplied by the priest. A wedding breakfast was unlikely. When they were asked how they proposed to celebrate, the young man said that his mother-in-law would give her daughter the run of the kitchen, and they would be able to have a meal together, just the two of them.

The priest felt desperately depressed by all this, and went to ask one of the neighbours if she could do anything to help. She was very touched, and answered, "Tell them to come here for dinner. I'm not a very good cook but I promise to do the very best I can." Her daughter was at the church door the next day, with a bouquet for the bride. The priest had gathered together a few young people, whom he knew, to sit in the front seats. As the young couple went up to the altar, the organ was playing. The carpet had been laid down, together with the best priedieux and chairs. You can imagine how happy they were. As he gave his short sermon, the priest saw the tears on their cheeks. In the sacristy afterwards, they said "We shall never forget this, Father".

Supposing this had been the sort of church where class distinctions count, and people who cannot afford anything better are married in some gloomy little corner . . . ! We cannot know the extent to which the Church can be disfigured and misrepresented in the eyes of those who watch her ministers and their conduct. We can clearly see, however, that a priest who does not think in terms of money, is, for the people who have the good fortune to know him, Christ, as they imagine him to be.

The priest's task is to witness for Christ in all possible circumstances. He can expect to come up against the same problems and rebuffs as his Master, because his task is to tell each man what the gospel demands of him. He will have to go to the defence of A. and that will annoy B. Even when he is right, it is possible that he will have no one on his side. His life is spent on razor-edged principles, with only God to guide and protect him.

It is not the priest's task to work out a happy medium between opposing political groups or between meanness and generosity, or laziness and excessive zeal, timidity and foolhardiness. The gospel is not a happy medium, and priests are not diplomats whose role is to conciliate, and concede and make everybody feel comfortable.

One Sunday I preached a sermon on the parable of the leaven in the dough. I wanted to suggest that the Church is not there to assure the permanence of existing institutions, but the development of all that is good in society. After the sermon, the president of a local committee (one of the more hidebound ones) came up to me and said I had upset one of the members by something I had said. "In fact he was rather annoyed", I was told. So I said "As far as that goes, our Lord upset one or two people himself. You can't tell the truth without annoying someone!". "Yes I know Father", he answered, "but my first responsibility is to our committee."

The priest's task is not to encourage complacency, but exactly the opposite. Evil must be shown for what it is, and men be put on their guard against it. The enemy is selfishness, and human weakness can bring this awful contamination into everything we do, even the best things we do. It can jeopardize the best of political programmes and falsify any legislation. When we preach the gospel and its demands on mankind, we are bound to unmask Pharisaism of many kinds, and to upset many good people entrenched in their complacency.

Our first task is to preach the whole gospel uncompromisingly. We cannot tone it down here and there, out of respect for those who may be disturbed by it, or to make it harmonize more easily with our own outlook. The cheering thing about the age in which we live is that it does appreciate honest and straightforward speaking. It is impressed by conviction and self-sacrifice. It is feverishly enthusiastic about causes, the more desperate the better, and preferably those which concern the have-nots, and other victims of society. If he refuses to come to terms with what is bad in the world in which he lives, any priest can be sure that he is doing his job, that he understands his parish, and that his parish understands him.

Chapter Eight

THE HEART OF A PRIEST

Priests make an implicit vow of celibacy. And so much has been written about their vow that you would think that there was no more to be said. Some people think of it as just another bit of hypocrisy that allows the ministers of the Catholic Church to avoid the burden of bringing up a family and providing for a wife and home. These people are usually prejudiced against clerical celibacy from the start, realizing that it involves a virtue that they would not presume to practise themselves.

Others, on the contrary, think that if the priest has set himself this ideal, he must be somehow out of reach of the sort of temptations that beset other people. They see him as a superhuman, ethereal creature poised between earth and heaven, and consequently exempt from the weaknesses and the sufferings of other people.

Thus we commonly find two opinions: either celibacy is impossible, or it is effortlessly easy. People are either on the look-out for the least sign of weakness in a priest, or they believe that human frailty can never touch him. The common factor in both these opinions is a refusal to condone the least slip in the matter of chastity. The layman's judgement in such matters can be inflexibly hard and demanding.

The truth of the matter is, of course, that a priest's celibacy is part of the priest's own complex human make-up. Consequently it is bound up in a host of normal difficulties of the sort that any human being has to face.

Only the Catholic Church has seen fit to impose celibacy on her ministers. The reason for this is because the Church counts on three things, namely the grace of God, the special grace of the priesthood and the generosity of the men who are chosen to be priests.

A priest is a man like any other man. There is a real sacrifice involved, and we have to face the facts. When a seminarian, let us say at the age of twenty-three, takes the sub-diaconate and makes his implicit vow of chastity, he knows what he is giving up, and he knows the struggle that he is accepting as a consequence of his sacrifice. He is not made differently from other men. He is flesh and blood, body and soul, and he has a heart that was made to love. Like any other man, he would be glad to be the father of a family. The fact that he renounces so much of the happiness that people of his age normally look forward to, makes him neither a masochist, nor an egoist. The truth is simply that he has chosen another ideal, an even greater and more wonderful ambition, to which he under-takes to devote all his love and all his life.

If he has any sense he will know already that there will always be a struggle for him. His parents have been telling him so all along. No one has been keeping him in the dark about what will happen. In fact everyone has made sure that he only takes up this career with his eyes open. There is a myth which claims that seminarians are forced into the priesthood. The truth is that all the seminary staff, all the spiritual directors, are constantly acquainting the seminarian with all the problems that lie in store. What would be the point in their inveigling any young man whom they suspected of not being able to keep his vow?

A young sub-deacon knows very well that there will be times when he will feel dreadfully alone, particularly at the end of some more than usually tiring, discouraging day. There will be no one there for him to confide in, no one who will listen with sympathy to the tale of his worries, or his hopes, or the things that give him happiness. He will see his brothers, and his school friends getting married, bringing up their families. He will be presented with nephews and nieces at the time of life when he might be having sons and daughters. He knows all this, and he knows that he must not be taken aback by a host of other temptations which at the moment he cannot even suspect. But the sacrifice he is making, is made with another family in view – that is the important thing. His task is a different one from that of his school friends and contemporaries. His whole life, and his whole heart, are to be dedicated to God and the service of mankind.

We admit that there are priests who disappoint and scandalize us. But what does this prove? Only the fact that the struggle that good priests put up must be a colossal one. It is foolish to claim that the Church demands too much in imposing celibacy on her clergy. Those who fall away are a very small minority indeed. The argument can be solved quite simply in the way that it was solved in a certain barracks, where a Catholic was told by a non-Catholic that he knew a priest who had fallen into sin. "Disgusting", he said, "because they have made a promise haven't they? Well they should damn well keep it!" (Incidentally, one usually finds that it is those who do not practise any religion who know these fallen priests, whereas people who really frequent their clergy very rarely know anything about the apostates) The Catholic answered, "All right, but it cuts both ways. What about all the married men you know? Do you think that they have nothing to be ashamed of, lots of them? They make a promise too, when they get married, to be faithful to one wife. If you were to count up the unfaithful husbands, there would be just no proportion between them and the unfaithful priests." But no one thinks of abolishing monogamy because married people are sometimes unfaithful to one another.

Why does the Church attach so much importance to the celibacy of the priest? Simply because she asks of him the complete gift of himself and his life. This means that he must be free from all other ties, so that nothing may take the place of God in his heart, and no one may have the right to monopolize the devotion that he owes to all his fellow men.

I once met three young Anglican clergymen, one in charge of a London parish, the other two about to leave for America where they were to begin a parish in a neglected coloured area. All three had decided to remain celibate so that they could devote more time to their parish work. When they told me of their decision, I felt, over and above the not unusual Anglo-Catholic yearning to be as Roman as possible, a real insight into the problem, making them accept of their own free will the law which the Catholic Church lays down for all her priests.

A Catholic priest gives up the possibility of having a family of his own, because he must be the father of a spiritual family, to which he must give all his love. Most people will never realize how much a priest is tied to his parish. From the moment he starts his ministry, a young priest's life, his hopes, his joys and his sorrows depend entirely on the triumphs and failures of his work. His life is, in essence, the life of the community in which he lives and labours. There is material for many more novels on the subject of the development of a young priest's work. In France, for instance, the young curates always look after the children, and the children will never know how their innocent remarks can grieve a priest who is young, untried, and trying desperately to give himself wholly to his young charges. They will never know what it means to him to receive their first confidences, when they turn to him for advice. Occasionally, when they have to face some crisis, they will learn that he takes them seriously, that he loses much sleep in trying to resolve their problems for them. Because he is responsible, he is conscious of his responsibility, and has to think of the consequences of what he may advise.

He begins to realize that he is in much the same position as a doctor, trying to diagnose an illness. Only he has to diagnose something interior, unseen except for certain odd indications. Like a young doctor, he is thrilled by the evidence of improvement, and terribly concerned by any sign of a relapse. Then, gradually, he learns that young people need not be taken quite as seriously as he thought. They are young, inclined to exaggerate. His failures, too, he can see as very minor catastrophes. But even though he eventually takes all these things in his stride, and evolves his own personal ways of dealing with the problems of others, he will, because he must, always keep the ability to *feel* their problems. He may become more competent, but he will always have to suffer, and hope, and sometimes fear.

Later on he will have to cope with the dramas that occur in marriages, and with all the difficulties of adult life. When the young curate has become a parish priest himself, it will be more than the children and the youth clubs that engage his apostolic zeal, it will be the whole parish with all its ups and downs.

Few people can know what it means to a priest when he comes to a new parish and asks himself the question; "Shall I be a success?" He is not thinking in terms of personal success, but of his responsibility of helping along the kingdom of God among these people. He knows very well that our Lord is doing all the real work but the question must remain, and does remain, "Shall I manage to understand them all? And will they like me?" It is not that he particularly desires to be loved and esteemed for himself, personally, but he knows perfectly well that if the people do take to him, everything will be much easier, and the kingdom of God will be the better off for it. But if he cannot find his way into their lives and their hearts, everything he says and does will be, to that extent, less effectual. So the kingdom of God does depend, in some proportion, on the way he goes about his work.

Admittedly the history of the Church, and the whole

unfolding of Christ's work of redemption, are certain in their outcome. There is no possibility of an ultimate tragic failure. But there certainly is drama and tragedy in many periods of the Church's history, in many places in which Christians have sought their redemption. So that in any one little corner of Christendom – a parish, for instance – the Christian drama is still in progress, and success and failure, in this place and at this moment of time, depend greatly on the success or the failure of the parish priest in his task.

Take a common situation like this one. A new priest arrives in a parish. No one has met him before. All the parishioners were used to the previous priest, and they liked him very much. The new priest is not envious of the old one. He has no need to be, since he knows that if they were good parishioners to some other priest, they can be equally good parishioners for him. So he does not set himself up as in any sense a competitor with his predecessor. But, even without wishing to, he is bound to discontinue certain past customs. And he is in duty bound, quite often, to break in on well-established habits of complacency. Then he can expect reactions! He is bound to be criticized and even calumniated. To start with, he is bound to be rather uncertain of the best way of doing things. Let him say a single word out of place and there will be plenty of observers to exaggerate his meaning out of all proportion.

The first few months are inevitably a trial, but even when he has become used to the place and the people, no priest can be completely at ease. His work is far too delicate to permit uninterrupted self-satisfaction. His work consists of advising people about the most intimate details of their lives, the most prized things for which they live. If people disagree with his methods they will do so vehemently, precisely because their private lives are involved. A priest's duty is to point out things that are bad, as well as approving the things which are good. If he should have to penalize a child in some way, or reprove someone for doing a job badly on his property, he will immediately find he has a faction against him somewhere in the parish. If he should have occasion to point out to a girl that her conduct is scandalous, her mother will come to the rescue and, from then on, be his sworn enemy. There is sure to come a time when he has to cross swords with someone involved in local labour problems, local politics, local property. Helpful parishioners will warn him not to provoke so and so too far. There are always plenty of Herods and Herodiases, and to push the analogy a stage further, there is a whole sideboard full of dishes ready and waiting for the parish priest's head!

Other trials are in store for the priest precisely on

account of the close ties which soon link him to his parish and his people. It will be very hard for him to leave if he has to go to another parish. When an official is given a change of post, he starts the same life over again in a new place, with his whole family still intact about him. But a priest's family is his parish. All those people whom he has cared for, both young and old, really are his children. When he has to leave them, it is very unlikely that he will see many of them again. Of course they will all say, "We'll come and see you, and of course you must come back sometimes and see us", but he knows very well that he will soon be forgotten. In fact he must be forgotten, simply because his successor must take his place entirely in the lives of these people. If he does keep in touch, he may even be meddling without knowing it, therefore it is best to keep away altogether. He cannot help suffering because he is, after all, a human being with a human heart; someone with feelings, attachments, and the ability to be tied up in other people's lives.

When he is tired and overworked, it is no wonder if he is sometimes overcome by loneliness. I remember the young priest who had a parish somewhere up in the mountains, who told me about the Christmas when, as he said, he was "the loneliest man in the whole parish. . . . Christmas night, and everyone so happy. I saw them all leave after Midnight Mass, and go home to their family celebrations. I couldn't sleep, I was so depressed in that empty house. I gave communion at seven next morning, then I had to rush off somewhere else for another Mass, then back to the parish church for High Mass. I got back to the presbytery at twelve. I lit the fire, cooked a bit of lunch, and all that afternoon I was absolutely alone."

He is a man, like any other. He has his faults and his failings. His character is no more perfect than yours. He can still be occasionally selfish, and self-indulgent, to the extent that he may, some day, neglect this or that part of his duty. Over and above this, which is normal enough in any life, there are special troubles inherent in his profession, which always threaten to do a great deal of damage.

He is a man in a position to direct others, and to tell others what to do. His authority must be exercised in the most private sphere of life – other people's consciences – where no one else has any authority. It is he who presides in his own church. In the sanctuary he is incensed like a prelate. Here is the danger of pride. He can become a kind of Jupiter, the kind of parish priest who orders everyone about, from the nuns to the sacristan. Such an authoritarian outlook is bound to be provocative, particularly in places where the people have lost contact with the Church and its pastors. Fortunately it has become a thing of the past for most of the younger clergy, but we can still find it without looking very hard. At a parish in

Brittany, for instance, a young priest was saying his first Mass, and his school friends had arranged an outdoor celebration. Dinner dragged on and on, presided over by the parish priest, and when it was suggested that it was time to join the party outside, he admonished the young priest in the following terms. "Now that you are a priest you must get into the habit of letting people wait for you. That will make them appreciate you all the more". No doubt he had very high ideals about the dignity of the priesthood, but these ideals have to conform to the gospel and to the present day.

A priest's work is always a delicate undertaking. He must always be on the look-out for other people's susceptibilities. Yet, while he is trying to be good and kind, he has to be careful not to overdo it, and become unctuous and over-indulgent. He has to be careful not to annoy people unnecessarily, but at the same time he must not be afraid to act and speak honestly. All the while he must guard against the temptation that comes with being able to organize his own life in the way that suits him best. His work cannot be checked by inspectors, and there is no material gain to act as an incentive. He can so easily get into the habit of taking things easily, being not lazy perhaps, but only half active, half alive.

Finally we have to remember that a priest ages more quickly than other people. His work is not in itself more demanding, more tiring, than that of others, but it does demand a mind that is especially wide-awake, and always ready to adapt itself to new conditions. A priest ages not so much because of his work as in relation to his work. His job depends so much on the qualities of his own person, his own reactions, his own reflections. He becomes more experienced as he gets older, we hope, and experience is more necessary than anything else in the business of looking after people's souls. But in an age like ours, when things change and develop so quickly, a priest is more than ever capable of getting quickly out of date. Every so often he has to readjust himself to what is new in society. Take a young curate at the end of the First World War. He understood the young people he had to look after then, but could he still understand them so easily by 1930? Ten years later, the situation was completely changed again. After the war, he had to make a real effort if he still wanted to talk in a way they could understand.

This is, after all, human nature. It cannot adapt itself, consequently we have to do something about it, all of us, when we are getting older. It is the normal thing. Little by little, we find the bold young man growing a little less bold, and someone who once lived in the future starts to live in the past. The man who was a leader for others tends to become the biggest hindrance to their making any further progress. Father is getting old, we hear, "*Il n'est plus dans la vie*". He's no longer with us! If he were a civil servant he would already have been given a pension. He would not have been given the opportunity to carry on, but forced to comply with the law and retire.

Alas, there is no law for the priest. He cannot be moved from his parish. That is his right, but what havoc it can cause in a parish! So often the priest is the last one to see that he is too old for the job. He struggles along bravely, wearily, ailing perhaps and no longer very firm on his feet. He screws up his courage and his remaining strength, and makes a terrific act of will just to show "brother ass" who is master. He wants to be of service to others right to the end, and he just cannot see that he has passed the stage when he can be of use to anyone. So we sometimes find large parishes looked after by octogenarians, still sticking to their responsibilities when their contemporaries in other walks of life have been enjoying their retirement for years.

Fortunately we do find that some old priests who can face the facts give a wonderful example. Perhaps these are the ones who were not quite so attached to the authority they held for so long. One does find, for instance, the old parish priest who petitions to give up his big city parish so that he can take up something less important in the country. Others have asked to be made curates again, others become convent chaplains or are content to confine themselves to preaching or some other specialized work.

Although by right no one can move a parish priest, he must examine his conscience, and realize he has a duty to resign when he is too old for his job. It needs a really strong character to make such a decision, particularly when a priest has been active all his life and feels that he still has much to give. The prospect of enforced idleness cannot be pleasant to such a man. It must be very hard to give up one's independence and become second in command to another, obeying, whereas one had hitherto given all the orders.

Worst of all he will be losing his family, the parish. These are his own people with whom he has become identified with the passing years. No one is surprised if a priest finds the sacrifice altogether too hard to make. When we leave a place in which we have been happy, it is as if some part of us had died. When a young priest goes from one parish to another, although the break is hard, he does at least know that he is going to start a new life. But for the old priest, who gives up for the last time, because he is old, or sick, such a departure can be like a foretaste of death.

It is nicer to die in harness, of course, which is what most of us want. That is the best time to go, if we must go, with all our loved ones round us. Far better this than retiring to a home for aged priests, with nothing but the promise of a gradual decline.

Life will go on in the parish which the old priest used to look after, and where he has left his heart after having given himself unsparingly. Others have taken his place, and perhaps there is hardly a soul there who remembers him any more. Perhaps his successors have made so many changes that no trace remains of his life and work. Now he is alone, although he is well looked after by the sisters, or some old servant, and his death will cause little stir in the community where he used to mean so much. Among the people whose lives he used to influence, the news that he is dead may be greeted with "Good heavens, I should have thought he'd died ages ago!" Some of them will come to the funeral, but not many.

This is all that we can see on the face of things. God sees beneath the surface. God knows that in those last years spent in retirement, he was glad to find that he had much more time for prayer. He was able to think more, and not only about the past. He went back to the slightly old fashioned piety he had been offered in his seminary days. He could spend all his time with God because he had so little contact now with the world. He was able to prepare for eternity and that, after all, is what old age is for. Old people are always a bit of a nuisance, a bit of a burden, inevitably, but if they are saints – people like the curé d'Ars, for instance – they are just as useful in old age as they were at the height of their powers. Their souls are no less powerful, now that their bodies are failing.

When an old priest thinks back on his seminary days, and in his last years finds the ideal of his youth shining more brightly, it may be a second childhood in the pejorative sense, but it is none the less that childhood ideal of the gospel, which is the highest of all ideals and a touchstone for eternal life. He can look back now on the whole span of life, from the first time when our Lord called him, while he was still a child perhaps, to the present moment when he can see clearly all that the Lord has done for him. He can only ask forgiveness for having been so unequal to the task. He knows he can say "I am an unprofitable servant", but he can add, "You made me a priest, Lord! It was your idea after all, and it was kind of you to pretend that you needed me."

[7]